BLESSED

RAISING TWO DAUGHTERS AS A SINGLE MUM WITH A DISABILITY

ESTHER SIMBI

ISBN: 978-1-922409-69-0
Published by Vivid Publishing
A division of Fontaine Publishing Group
P.O. Box 948, Fremantle
Western Australia 6959
www.vividpublishing.com.au

NATIONAL
LIBRARY
OF AUSTRALIA

A catalogue record for this
book is available from the
National Library of Australia

Some names of people in this book have been changed.

CONTENTS

FOREWORD

It was 2006 when I met this incredible young woman named Esther Simbi. My name is Stan Lewinski and I am a friend and mentor to Esther.

The chance meeting occurred at the Australian Migrant Resource Centre (AMRC) where Esther was doing her placement requirements for a Social Work degree and where I was employed in various capacities. The AMRC is a not-for-profit organisation for the settlement of asylum seekers and people from refugee backgrounds.

I noticed Esther immediately, apart from her obvious disability, by her exuberant demeanour, keenness to learn and self-confidence in a quiet manner. Also, her name Esther was the same as my late sister, with whom I had a close relationship. In the first instance, I did not want to become personally involved but after some time it became evident that, although fiercely independent, Esther needed some help in establishing her domesticity due to her post-polio syndrome.

As time passed, I could not help but be impressed by her determination to overcome the challenges she faced on a daily basis and her positivity to succeed in achieving her goals and dreams. In her first book, *Beyond Calamity*, Esther described in much detail the hardships and trauma she overcame in Africa and now, in this sequel, this inspirational woman continues with her journey in her new homeland, Australia.

Although most grateful for all the help she received during her settlement years, Esther nevertheless initially faced many traumas and heartaches: the deaths of her stillborn child and of her beloved mother, battling and overcoming relationship hardships, bullying and discrimination in the workplace, her ongoing health problems, an unfair employment dismissal, frequent falls, getting around generally without a wheelchair, the stigma of having a disability, and the lack of support from some members of her own community.

Yet Esther's positivity and sheer determination to overcome these difficulties has led to her pursuing her goals and dreams. Just some of her achievements are completing a Bachelor's degree in Social Work and a Master's degree in Mediation and Conflict Resolution; gaining employment as a social worker, case manager, service coordinator, intake coordinator, project coordinator and facilitator; obtaining her driver's licence; running for parliament in 2014 and 2018 for the Dignity Party SA;

conducting many speaking engagements; advocating for social justice as the founder of the Crossing the Bridge Project, which aims to support African women and children with disabilities; and raising two beautiful daughters single-handedly.

How inspirational! Not bad for a young South Sudanese woman from a refugee background with a disability. I feel privileged to have played a miniscule part in Esther's life and wish her all the success with her second book, which I am certain will inspire you.

Stan Lewinski

Acknowledgements

A big thank you to Stan Lewinski for writing the foreword to this book, for being a good friend and a mentor.

A big thank you to David Ayambo and Dominic Moi for your cultural insight and relationship advice.

A big thank you to my friends, Karen Forde and Kristy, for your ongoing support with looking after my children whenever I need it.

A big thank you to my sister Angelina for your ongoing support.

A big thank you to my support workers, Patty, Helen, Tanya, Harjot, Trish, Gail and Hye Jin, for supporting me in my house with daily living tasks that I would not have been able to complete on my own without your help.

A big thank you to my support worker Patrober Kemboi for helping me with looking after my children in my house on weekends to enable me to write this book. Without your support, I would not have been able to write this book as quickly as I have.

A big thank you to Lutheran Disability Services SA, Community Support Inc. SA and to Hessel Group SA for providing my support.

A big thank you to Liellie McLaughlin for your support in promoting my first book, *Beyond Calamity*.

A big thank you to Deng Enoch, Celian Kidega, Cathi Tucker and the South Sudanese community in Adelaide for your support during my book launch for my first book in June 2019 and for making my book launch a success.

A big thank you to the Australian government for your continuous support in my life and in my family's life.

A big thank you to the National Disability Insurance Scheme for funding my supports.

A big thank you to the Aboriginal Kaurna people for allowing me to live on their Kaurna land.

A big thank you to Fontaine Publishing Group for publishing this book and for getting this book out into the hands of our readers.

And to you my beautiful daughters, Destiny and Dorcas, this book is dedicated to you. Thank you for bringing so much joy into my life. Love always, Mum.

One

INTRODUCTION

My name is Esther Simbi. I was born in Kajo-Keji, South Sudan, to a poor peasant family. I don't know what year I was born. It was a home birth in the village with no birth certificate and my mother didn't remember the exact year. The year of my birth on my visa for Australia is 1977. I don't look or feel forty-three years old so I have calculated and guessed my age to be a more realistic thirty-nine years old. Unfortunately, I have not been able to change this in Australia because I don't have a birth certificate to prove my age. If I was four years old when I contracted poliomyelitis in 1985, then I am thirty-nine years old now.

Apart from being a peasant, my father was also a primary school teacher at Beliyak Primary School in

Kajo-Keji and he also worked as a cleaner in Mundari Hospital in Kajo-Keji. My mother didn't have the opportunity to pursue education due to South Sudanese cultural practices, where women are trained to be housewives, mothers and family/community carers.

It is clear that I am not from a family of writers, nor from a family of academics. I was not in a position to follow my parents' career paths like other children do because neither of my parents was a social worker, a mediator or an author. I took my own career path, followed my instincts and dreams, and I became a social worker, a mediator and now a published author. God raised me from the ashes to be all that I am today for his own Glory and I can't thank God enough for his Grace. When God opens a door, no human will ever be able to close it (Revelations 3:7–8 and Isaiah 22:22), no matter how hard they try, and when God says yes, nobody can say no (2 Corinthians 1:20). I am the first woman in my family and in my community to have ever published a book, to have ever graduated from university with a Master's degree, and to have ever run for Parliament in Australia. My encouragement to anyone reading this book is that you don't have to have a beautiful beginning to have a beautiful ending. It doesn't matter who you are, where you are in life, where you have been and where you have come from, you can start from where you are now and your story will have a successful and a beautiful ending. How your story starts does not matter but how your story ends is what counts.

I am the youngest of six children and I am from the South Sudanese Kuku community. I speak the Kuku language and English. My parents were divorced when I was four years old and my mother went to live with her relatives in a village called Lomura in Kajo-Keji, leaving me and my siblings with my father. My two brothers ran away from home when I was a baby due to domestic violence. In South Sudanese culture, children belong to their father. In any case of marriage or family breakdown, the woman will leave without her children and that was exactly what my mother did. My three sisters and I were reunited with our mother a few months later when our father took ill and was unable to care for us. A few weeks after settling in at my mother's village, I contracted polio-myelitis. One morning in Lomura village, I woke up with a high fever and a body paralysed from neck to toe. I was not able to stand or sit up. My mother gave me a medicine made from local herbs, and she invented her own form of physiotherapy treatment where she massaged my body in cold water every morning. She also tied my arms to two poles to support me, and she left me to stand there for an hour every morning and evening for two to three months. I had to learn to sit and to walk again, and I eventually regained strength in my upper body. Thanks to my mother, who worked tirelessly, I was able to walk again, though with great difficulty.

When I was born there was no immunisation against

polio available for children in South Sudan. I was left with a weak lower back, a deformed and painful right foot, and a very weak left leg. My left leg is two inches shorter than my right leg which makes balancing difficult when walking. I bend forward when walking, putting a lot of strain and pain on my right leg and lower back. I now suffer from the late effects of polio called post-polio syndrome, which is associated with headaches, muscle aches, bone and joint pain, fatigue and general body exhaustion. I limp when walking and I have a lot of falls causing injuries. In December 2015 when I was pregnant with my now four-year-old daughter, I had a fall and fractured my left ankle. Wearing a plaster for six weeks meant that I had to learn to walk again as the plaster had weakened my left leg muscles even more. I now have a lot of pain in my right knee because of falling and landing on it most of the time and I am on a waiting list for surgery on my right knee. I was on medication to manage the pain, which was a short-term fix, and went off the medication following a cortisone injection in my right knee in January 2020, which has worked a little bit, but I will still need to see the orthopaedic surgeon to discuss the next step.

I use a wheelchair outside of the house to access the community and sometimes in the house depending on how I am feeling on the day. On some days my legs are very weak, especially when the weather is too hot or too cold, making my mobility very difficult even for a very short distance or even for a minute. I try not to use the wheelchair much, though, to keep my muscles strong and active. I use my left arm to push my left knee back when I am walking for balance to aid my mobility. I have now damaged my left elbow because of the way I walk and now I am waiting for surgery to fix my left elbow. The front bones in my left elbow have spilt, causing my elbow to lock itself. My elbow is not flexible anymore and every time I move my left arm, one bone in my elbow presses down on a nerve, causing numbness in my middle, ring and pinky fingers. In mid-2015 I fell in the kitchen and hit my left elbow first on the kitchen bench and then on the floor really hard, which has also aggravated the pain in my left elbow. Writing can sometimes become difficult due to the pain in my elbow.

I now have a specialised, above-the-knee leg brace for my left leg from the Queen Elizabeth Hospital in Adelaide, funded by the National Disability Insurance Scheme (NDIS), which I love. I have been going for walks in it which is helping with balancing. It has also taken off the pressure in my left elbow. When I was young, my leg muscles were stronger and I was able to walk for ten to fifteen minutes without resting, but after I turned twenty-five here in Australia, my muscles started to weaken. Now I cannot walk for five minutes without resting and falling. The older I get, the weaker my legs and lower back get and I am finding that I am using the wheelchair more than I did four years ago.

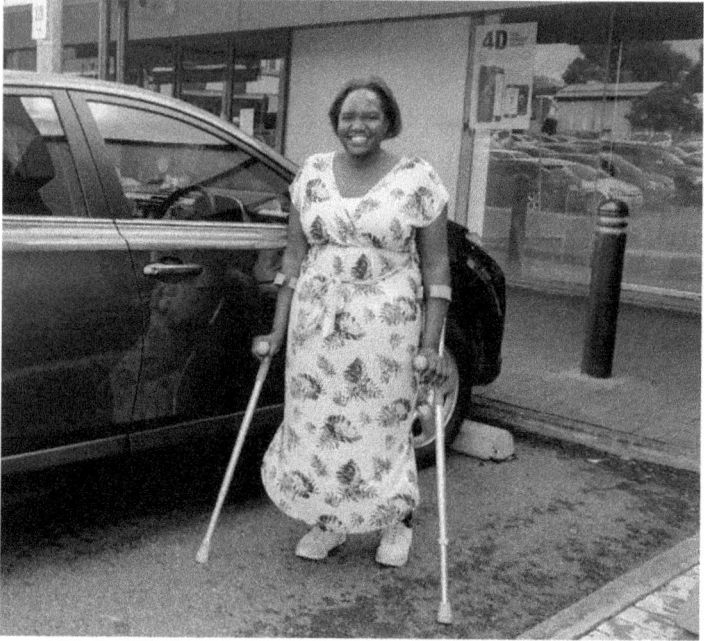

Esther standing with elbow crutches next to her car
at a Kmart carpark in Adelaide

The sight in my left eye is slightly weaker than the sight in my right eye. I also choke while swallowing and I now see a speech pathologist funded by the NDIS to manage my swallowing. The speech pathologist identified that the polio had weakened my swallowing muscles in my neck, and this explains why I am always choking while swallowing. My speech therapist has helped design strategies for me to use at home to manage my swallowing, which is working for now. I was diagnosed with post-polio syndrome here in Australia fourteen years ago, which can only be managed by resting and not overworking my muscles.

I am a single mother of two beautiful daughters: Destiny, aged ten, and Dorcas, aged four. I lost my middle daughter, Hannah, to stillbirth in June 2015. I named my third daughter Dorcas, which is a Bible name, in memory of Hannah. I could have named her Tabitha or any other name but I instead chose Tabitha's second name, Dorcas, which fits well with the memory of my second daughter. Many people have asked me why I named my third daughter Dorcas of all names. Others have said that she will be bullied at school because of her name and that people might call her Dorc or 'dorky', which is not nice. I also get asked a lot why I named my first daughter Destiny instead of Rebekah, Erica, Hope or Willow? My response is that, unless you have experienced what I have been through in my young life, you will not understand the reasons why I have chosen to name my daughters Destiny and Dorcas. For you to understand the meaning of the name Dorcas, please read the Bible, Acts 9:36–42.

Esther and her daughters at their church carpark in
Adelaide in January 2020

My family and I fled the Sudan civil war and we
resettled in Uganda, where I grew up in three different
refugee camps for nineteen years before migrating to
Australia in July 2005 as a refugee. I completed a Bachelor

of Social Work in 2007 and a Master of Mediation and Conflict Resolution in 2014 at the University of South Australia. I worked with the South Australian Department of Child Protection (formerly known as Families SA) and the Department for Human Services (formerly known as Disability SA) from December 2007 to July 2013 as a social worker, case manager, service coordinator, intake coordinator, telephone counsellor and facilitator. In 2014 I founded, and was the coordinator of, the Crossing the Bridge Project, which was aimed at supporting African women with disabilities, mothers of African children with disabilities and the wives and female family members of African men with disabilities in South Australia. I ran for Parliament with Dignity Party SA (formerly known as Dignity for Disability) in the Upper House as a lead candidate in the 2014 state election and I was also on the Dignity Party's Upper House ticket for the 2018 state election, representing people with disabilities in South Australia. I was the first African woman from a refugee background to run for Parliament not only in South Australia, but Australia wide.

Two

REFUGEE WOMEN IN REFUGEE CAMPS

Being a refugee woman means to be tortured, raped, stigmatised, traumatised and disadvantaged. Like other refugee women in the world who often experience the unnatural deaths of numerous family members, including children, husbands and other male supporters, such as fathers and brothers, during a war, I lost my father, a brother and a sister during the Sudan civil war. Not only that, I also experienced a loss of identity, homeland, culture and social status. I came to Australia as a stateless refugee but I am now glad to be an Australian citizen and I am proud to call myself a South Sudanese Australian. Because one brother as well as my father were killed during the civil war and because my other brother remained in South Sudan, my mother, my sisters and I found ourselves fleeing South Sudan to seek refuge in Uganda without the protection and support of a male relative. This exposed me and my family to torture and trauma in Ugandan refugee camps.

Life in a refugee camp is not any easier for any refugee woman as she might be exposed to danger, rape, starvation and death. Refugee women may find themselves the primary caregivers of their family, responsible for the care of their children, the sick, those with disabilities and elderly family or community members, which is exactly what happened to my mother. Their time is occupied with the most basic tasks of survival — finding food, water, firewood for cooking, medicine / local herbs and shelter. In Kyangwali refugee camp in Uganda, for example, South Sudanese refugee women were often forced into low-skilled jobs, including selling their farm produce to earn money to buy meat, fish and other things to feed their children. There are limited opportunities for training and education for refugee women and their children in the refugee camps, though some women would be lucky to secure employment from refugee organisations in the camps. I was one of those few refugee women employed in the camps as a primary school teacher. Some employment in the camps had such low pay and the conditions of the work were so tough that prostitution became a more viable option for some refugee women. Some women would be sexually exploited by their employers before they even started working on the job and before they were paid. Promotion to a higher level and salary increase for some refugee women would also purely be based on sexual exploitation.

Some refugee women who are not lucky enough to attain employment in the camps because of very limited or no English skills would choose to send their daughters to be sexually exploited by authorities in the camps or in their country of refuge in order to earn a living. Having said this, some African girls choose to prostitute themselves to earn money regardless of their family status. All risk contracting sexually transmitted diseases, such as gonorrhoea, syphilis and HIV/AIDS. Other girls would become pregnant, while others would die. When a refugee girl becomes pregnant as a result of sexual exploitation, her or her family's problems will not end but, rather, increase as the fathers of those children will not take any responsibility, in spite of their wealth.

Although some refugee women wait for a peaceful repatriation when hostilities in their country end, many refugee women in the camps hope to obtain asylum in a Western country. For a few, like me, their dream of being resettled in the Western world, such as in Australia, becomes a reality. But even the quest to obtain asylum becomes problematic when the refugee camp is located in a country where corruption is endemic. Not only that, in other cultures and refugee camps, for instance, it is extremely difficult for a woman to move freely in the camp or in the residential area. These reasons and other issues, including language barriers and cost of transport, make it even harder for some refugee women to access foreign embassies or the UNHCR office in the area to register their refugee status. Even if refugee women are lucky enough to reach those centres, they may face corrupt male officials who will only process their claim in return for bribes or sex. For an empty-handed refugee woman like I was, money for bribes is impossible to procure. As a result, many refugee women stay in camps for many years and are cut off from the world. I call myself one of the lucky and blessed refugee women because I was able to obtain asylum status from Kyangwali refugee camp using a support letter provided to me by the head of Makerere Institute of Professionals in Uganda, where I completed my social work diploma. The support letter saved me from paying bribery money or from any sexual exploitation while I was being processed in the camp to be resettled. I am also blessed to have been resettled in Australia, which has enabled me to escape torture and trauma, and the risk of being cut off from the rest of the world.

Both in exile and in the war-torn country, refugee women's physical health deteriorates significantly; however, the extent of these problems differ from one refugee camp to the next and from one country to another. There are a number of factors that contribute to women's poor health and these include pre-existing problems, culture, religion and level of international support. In-adequate diet, chronic malnutrition, chronic infectious diseases, including tuberculosis and other airborne diseases, repeated pregnancies, and unhealthy and poor-hygiene environments are also the cause of much ill health in refugee women living in refugee camps. Other factors involved in poor health are overcrowded living conditions, poor working conditions and lack of access to immunisation as well as lack of health-care facilities and education in refugee camps. Not only that, refugee women have less access to medical facilities in the camps than men as most medical practitioners in the camps are men and in many Islamic cultures, for example, it is unacceptable for a female patient to see a male doctor. Refugee women also experience a high level of sexually transmitted diseases and cervical cancer due to lack of screening facilities in the camps and in their war-torn countries of origin.

High mortality and morbidity during childbirth are common both in refugee camps and in war-torn countries due to lack of professional assistance and proper hygiene practices during childbirth. Because there is a lack of medical facilities in the refugee camps, most refugee women have their babies at home whether they are in refugee camps or internally displaced in their war-torn countries of origin. In some instances, home or village childbirth may go wrong, which may result in the deaths of women or their babies. Although some refugee women may access support from home/village midwives who might also be relatives, often the people helping deliver babies in the refugee camps or in the villages in their war-torn countries of origin do not have sufficient training as midwives. Even if they have proper health training, lack of medical facilities and equipment may also result in death during childbirth.

Many refugee women from Africa experience the cruel practice of female genital mutilation (FGM), which is a very traumatic procedure usually performed without anaesthetic and in poor sanitary conditions. Many refugee women who have experienced FGM suffer lifelong health problems, such as repeated urinary tract infections, stones in the urethra and bladder, growth of scar tissue at the site, chronic pelvic infection resulting from obstructed menstrual flow and psychological torture. Some of these women also experience difficulties during childbirth and they suffer lifelong mental illness.

Refugee women can suffer from a variety of psychological problems, ranging from minor anxiety and depression to severe post-traumatic stress disorder, sometimes with associated psychosis. In cases of rape and sexual assault, feelings of dirtiness, fear, flashbacks, nightmares, powerlessness, worthlessness, shame, embarrassment, guilt, loss of confidence and very low self-esteem, depression and anxiety are predominant. Many survivors of rape experience various gynaeco-logical problems, including excessive and very painful menstruation or, in some instances, absence of menstruation. These problems may be a result of psychological distress. Psychological problems among refugee women are often expressed in the form of physical problems where cultural expression becomes inappropriate. Refugee women also experience intense bereavement, grief and loss over the deaths of loved ones and disconnection from their country of origin and family/community support network. The absence of professional counselling services in the refugee camps and in other communities, for example the South Sudanese community, often results into ongoing psychological distress. Where counselling services are available, some refugee women whether in camps or not tend to underestimate or ignore their mental health problems, due to cultural beliefs that people should not talk about their personal and family issues to professionals and non-family members; being preoccupied with poor or ongoing physical health issues; and the urgency of meeting basic survival needs. Counselling may also not be available in the woman's own language, which may hinder some refugee women from accessing assistance.

Refugee women who are granted refugee status in a new country like Australia often arrive with the hope of putting together the shattered pieces of their lives. Yet they now face the daunting task of adapting to a new culture and society that is very different to anything they have ever known. Refugee women can find themselves being overwhelmed with a number of settlement issues, including language difficulties, domestic violence, financial problems and lack of knowledge about public transport, housing, employment, the legal system, education and other services. While refugee men have greater opportunities to socialise and learn the language of their new country, refugee women are often left isolated, looking after their children and completing house chores. They have also lost the traditional social support provided by their extended family network and at social gatherings. Continuation of war in their homeland, as in South Sudan, destruction of their community, concern about family members scattered all over the world and changes in the structure of their family are other challenges faced by refugee women in a new country like Australia. Single refugee mothers and single mothers from a refugee background like myself also carry the burden of raising their children single-handedly without any family support network around them. Refugee women may also be forced to work in low-skilled jobs, as in the refugee camps, in the Western countries they have resettled in to support their families.

Some refugee women become the victims of domestic violence as their husbands, who are also deeply traumatised, are unable to control their anger and may subject their family to violence. In many instances, domestic violence is not spoken about as some refugee women do not speak English, do not know their rights in their new country and they may have come from cultures where women are considered the property of their husbands and thus are unable to complain. In Western countries, refugee women find themselves coping not only with their own past traumatic memories and experiences, but also the ongoing trauma of their husbands' violence and post-migration living difficulties as well as family and marriage breakdown issues. There is a high level of family/marriage breakdown among South Sudanese families in Australia, my own marriage breakdown included, compared to back home in South Sudan or in Uganda, but these issues are often swept under the carpet because of South Sudanese cultural practices and due to language barriers. Outspoken South Sudanese women like me who are trying to raise awareness and hopefully address some of the issues that South Sudanese women are experiencing in Australia are often thought to be spoiled and nobody from the community will listen to them. Hopefully this book will help raise awareness, not only in the South Sudanese community but also in the wider community. There is no doubt that refugee women have special needs and require ongoing specialised assistance from torture and trauma treatment services in their new country.

Three

MY JOURNEY TO AUSTRALIA

Esther in a friend's house in 2006, wearing the
same clothes she wore on her flight to Australia

I went to Kyangwali refugee camp in Hoima, Western Uganda, in December 2002. My first offshore resettlement interview there was to be resettled in the United Kingdom but when my sister Angelina in Australia found out, she refused to let me go to the UK. Instead, she asked me to leave Kyangwali refugee camp at once, go to Ibakwe refugee camp where my mother was living to collect my mother and then go to Kampala to begin the resettlement process to Australia with my mother. I left Kyangwali in the middle of the night and I went to Kampala. I didn't go to Ibakwe refugee camp straight away, as my sister had instructed, but I instead completed the Australian visa application forms in Kampala and posted them to Australia. The plan was for me to wait in Kampala until an opportunity became available for my mother and I to attend an immigration interview and then I could go and collect her from Ibakwe. I was not able to provide food for my mother and me in Kampala for a period of over six months, and my sister in Australia could not afford to provide for us in Kampala for over six months either, so my mother had to remain in Ibakwe refugee camp and I stayed in Kampala until we were shortlisted for an immigration interview. That was when I went to Ibakwe refugee camp to collect her.

As you will soon learn in this book, life became very hard for my mother and me in Kampala due to lack of food. While I was waiting for our immigration interview,

I took a job in a paint company in Kampala as a store manager, a staff supervisor and as a stock holder. I worked for three months to start with but I was paid only one month's salary, which was not even enough to reimburse me for the cost of transport for the three months to travel to my job. I borrowed the money for transport from a friend. Because I was the only highly educated employee in the company at that time and because I was the only manager there at the time, my friend and I thought that I was going to be paid a higher salary but I was instead paid the lowest salary in the company. Even lower than the junior customer service employee's salary just because I was a South Sudanese refugee woman with a disability in Uganda. After I received my first payment, I submitted my resignation letter to Mike, the business owner, who claimed that he didn't know that I had not been paid the salary I was entitled to. He pleaded with me to continue working in his company and said he would sort my payments out with the accountant, Betty, who was also his niece. Mike said that I was the only highly educated, genuine and hardworking employee he had ever had and that he did not want to lose me. I was also the only employee he could trust, mainly because I was from a different culture with extremely hard life experiences which, in his opinion, had shaped my life choices. Mike didn't know how to read and write in English because he never went to school. He was confident that I would not lie to him or hide anything from him, which is why he wanted to keep me around for longer. I had been referred to his company by a Pastor in Uganda who was like a mother to Mike and me, and Mike feared creating any tension between me, him and the Pastor. It turned out that the money Mike had used to open the paint business had been given to him by the same Pastor who referred me to work there.

I later found out that Betty was busy with her university exams and that she had used some of my money on personal things because Mike had been sick in the hospital and that was the only money she had at hand. When asked why she took money from my salary and not from the other employees' salaries, Betty responded that I was humble, polite, patient and trustworthy and she was confident that I wouldn't fight her or take the matter any further because of my disability. And because I was a refugee in Uganda, Betty didn't think that I would win if I took the case any further.

I worked for two more months and I was paid one month's salary again. This time there was a new accountant, Alice, who had worked with the company for many years as a senior customer service officer. Mike summoned me and Alice into his office after my second complaint. I arrived in Mike's office first and Alice arrived a few minutes later. Alice sat on Mike's lap, kissed him and said, 'Yes honey, you sent for me?' Mike said, 'Yes and please sit down.' Alice sat on the chair next to Mike and Mike asked her what had happened to my payments. Alice was quiet for a few moments and then she responded, telling Mike that she would crosscheck and get back to him. She promised to pay me any outstanding payments the next day in full.

After I returned to my desk, Alice followed me to my office and threatened to 'destroy' my life and make me 'disappear' if I ever mentioned to anyone, including Mike's niece, what had happened in his office or if I ever made any more complaints to Mike again! I was so angry, hurt and ashamed by Alice's behaviour. She said that Mike was her husband and that there was nothing I could do to make him pay my salary in full unless she said so. As far as I knew, Alice was not married to Mike and had never been in any form of relationship with him, nor was she with any man at the time. She was a single mother. All I knew was that she was angry because I had been given the manager's and the supervisor's job and not her. She had been working with the company for a very long time before I joined and she thought that, because she was one of the first employees, she would automatically be promoted to the store manager or supervisor role. I feared for my life because Alice was from the witchcraft-practising and human-eating tribe in Uganda so I cleared my desk as fast as I could and left the office immediately without waiting to be paid.

A few weeks later, I was sick with typhoid malaria and I was admitted to a medical centre in Kampala. The doctor there asked me to pay a big amount of money before my treatment could begin. I rang Mike and told him that I was sick and I needed money to pay for my medical bills. Could he please pay the rest of my salary? Mike told me that he would send Betty with money right away. He also said that I should return to work when I was feeling better. I waited that day but Betty didn't come and then I remembered a lady I helped in Kyangwali refugee camp who told me that if I ever needed help with anything in Kampala, I should contact her brother Alfred. I rang Alfred and asked if he could help me with some money to pay for my treatment and I would pay him back when I was feeling better. Alfred, who owned a retail shop in Kampala, came to the medical centre with food and drinks, and he paid my medical bills in full. I was discharged three days later and Alfred transported me back home to where I was living. He also gave me money for food. Later that day, Betty came to my house with two months salary. She apologised and informed me that Alice had been sacked from the company following her performance in Mike's office in my presence.

Betty rang her uncle while she was in my house and her uncle pleaded with me to go back to work. A few days later, I went to the immigration office in Kampala and discovered that a date and time for my interview had been scheduled. I had no time to waste but to go to Ibakwe refugee camp and collect my mother at once. The day of our interview arrived and we attended the immigration office without an interpreter. It was around 10am on a Wednesday morning. After the interview, the Australian interviewer asked my mother and me to wait for the outcome outside of the interview room. At about 3pm, my name was called and we went back to the interview room where we were informed that we were successful. I couldn't contain my emotions and I burst into tears while my mother prayed. I was crying tears of joy.

The following day, we went back to the immigration office and started stage one of our immigration medical examination process. In the weeks that followed, we attended a series of medical examinations. There was one particular physical examination that I thought was inappropriate where refugees, including myself, were asked to strip naked in front of the white doctor examiners. I didn't understand what the doctors were looking for and why this examination was required. All I knew was that some people, mostly men, were not allowed to migrate to Australia either because they were circumcised or because they had scarring on their bodies. The immigration medical examiners alleged that those men with big scars were soldiers or had been involved in the Sudan civil war, and that South Sudanese men who were circumcised were Muslims and they could pose a threat in Australia, and they were failed in the medical examinations. God was on our side and my mother and I passed our medical examinations.

Our medical forms were sent to Sydney but not all the forms were sent. A few months later, I went to the immigration office where I was informed that my mother and I would need to do more medical examinations for our visa to be granted because not all of our forms had been received in Australia. I started following this up in Uganda to find out what had happened to our medical forms. The woman handling our forms found out that part of our forms were in a draw somewhere in her office at the immigration office. She couldn't explain how those forms had travelled from the medical examination centre to her office about sixteen kilometres away. She also could not explain how the forms had been taken out of their envelopes and ended up in her office drawer. The forms were quickly posted to Sydney and in May 2005 we received confirmation that our visas to Australia had been granted and that our air tickets had been booked for July. We had one more thing left to do, which was to attend an orientation about Australia before our flight. The orientation took two days and I couldn't have been happier.

We were not provided with transport, food or money for accommodation during our interview, medical examination and orientation period. The woman providing the orientation was not Australian. The orientation started at 7am and finished at 6pm. We were given a two-hour lunch break. There was no breakfast, no morning tea, no lunch, no water and no afternoon tea provided. I later learnt that some people, especially Ugandans who had applied to be resettled in Australia as South Sudanese refugees and some South Sudanese friends of people working at the immigration office in Uganda, had been provided with transport money, food and accommodation in Kampala city from the time of their interview to the time they flew out to Australia, because they knew how the system worked and they asked for that support. Some of them even stayed in expensive hotels in Kampala near the immigration office for more than six months while real refugees like me suffered with no food, no proper accommodation and no transport money, despite being entitled to it. The money provided to assist refugees while they waited for their visas was mismanaged by immigration staff on the ground in Uganda. The relief aid provided by UNHCR to help refugees in refugee camps in Uganda was also mismanaged by some Ugandans and refugee helpers on the ground. I urge the government of Australia to reopen all the rejected South Sudanese refugee visa applications and re-examine them carefully. The government should also send Australians to conduct offshore immigration interviews, medical examinations and orientations about Australia to prevent further mismanagement of funds and aid.

While I was waiting for my visa and flight, I took a job in a hair salon near where I lived but again I was paid very little money, not even enough to buy a meal for two, so I quit the hair salon job. I returned to work with the paint company for two months. This time I was paid every month but still not paid in full. I was lucky that I had my sister in Australia who supported my mother and me with finances whenever she could. During this period, my mother and I ate rice and beans on a daily basis as this was the only food we could afford. Sometimes we ate fish, meat with vegetable, and green bananas (matoke) if we had money from my sister.

The day of our flight to Australia arrived and we still had to find money to hire a taxi to get to the immigration office. Even though the staff at the immigration office had vans to transport refugees from where they were staying to the office and then to the airport, we were not provided with that transport service and we had to find our own way of getting ourselves and our luggage to the office. I am aware of some South Sudanese refugees whose applications for resettlement in the West were successful but missed their flights because they were unable to afford to stay in Kampala, so they stayed far away from the city and they missed their flights as a result. These South Sudanese refugees were either unaware that their visas had been granted and their flights had been booked or they were simply unable to transport themselves to the immigration office in time.

When we arrived at the immigration office that evening, we were given instructions on how to get ourselves safely to Australia and not be left behind either in Nairobi, Kenya, or Johannesburg in South Africa. The immigration staff transported my mother and me to Entebbe airport but they left us in the carpark with our immigration documents and luggage. They returned a few minutes later and a staff member checked us in and then she left. It was 12am Uganda time, Wednesday 6 July 2005. A family friend of ours who came to the airport separately to say goodbye to us helped carry our luggage to the check-in point and waited until we had checked in. When we got to the border security area, he left. We got into a small aeroplane and flew to Nairobi and then to Johannesburg in a much bigger aeroplane. The staff at Entebbe airport, in Nairobi and in Johannesburg treated us very well. They gave us breakfast in Entebbe airport at 3am before we got on the plane and we were also given morning tea at the airport in Nairobi free of charge but I couldn't eat much. A woman at Johannesburg provided us with a big lunch of charcoal chicken, she checked us in and she walked my mother and I to the Qantas entrance then she left. I had never seen nor ever been closer or inside such a huge aeroplane before in my life. Because of my disability, my mother and I were given the access seats in the plane. Unfortunately, this was also an area for families with young children who cried and made a lot of noise all the way to Sydney. My flight was not comfortable because of the noise from the young children and because I was scared of flying. I started throwing up from 10pm the previous night, before we went to the immigration office in Kampala, until we arrived in Sydney. I didn't vomit much on the plane but I was weak, tired and hungry. I didn't want to eat anything because I feared that I would vomit even more on the plane.

We arrived in Sydney at 10am and waited until 4pm for our flight to Adelaide. I don't remember the exact time we checked in to fly to Adelaide, but I do remember that we arrived at Adelaide airport at 6pm on Thursday 7 July 2005. Many people from the South Sudanese community in Adelaide came to the airport to welcome us. They were singing, dancing and drumming. There was even more singing and dancing in my sister's house when we got there. There were many people in my sister's house to welcome us, to pray for us and to have dinner together with us. There was plenty of food in my sister's house. I was very tired and weak from the flight and from the vomiting so I didn't eat much and I went to bed. When I woke up the following morning, everybody was gone.

Four

OVERCOMING RESETTLEMENT CHALLENGES IN AUSTRALIA

Esther at a shopping centre carpark in
Adelaide leaning on her first car in 2007

Very early the following day, my sister took my mother and me to open our bank accounts and to register with Centrelink. She also took us to register with the Families SA office, where we were provided with public transport concession cards. She took us to the Australian Refugee Association (ARA) office to receive assistance with furniture, and to the Salvation Army to collect some food and clothes vouchers, and she also took us to the Vinnies charity shop to collect some clothes. My first day in Australia was a very busy one but I got to rest that weekend and on the days that followed. A few days after we arrived in Australia, a social worker from ARA came to my sister's house to conduct an assessment to determine what support I would require as a person with a disability. As you will soon find out in this book, this social worker would later help me resettle after everyone in my community in South Australia turned their backs on me.

My sister helped us secure a two-bedroom private rental accommodation for my mother and me to move into, but before we moved in, my sister and I had a disagreement over something and she threw me out of her house. Only three weeks after arriving in Australia, I found myself all alone in the new rental property and in a new country. But at least I had Jane there to help me with grocery shopping and resettlement orientation. Jane gave me her phone number to ring her if I needed help with anything or if I was stuck somewhere and needed transport to get back home. Jane also wrote down for me the bus numbers to catch to go to the city and then to the ARA office and to get back home.

As part of my punishment for not agreeing with her in what she wanted us to do, my sister refused to have my mother move in with me so I was faced with having to pay the expensive rent by myself. I also had to pay back the money (over $2,000) that the immigration office had lent to my sister for our air tickets. At the time, I was receiving Newstart Allowance of $360 a fortnight from the welfare agency (Centrelink), which was not enough to pay the rent, let alone paying bills. The rent was $375 a fortnight. I didn't know that I could apply for rental assistance from Centrelink but after I moved to the disability housing I mention later, I was successfully able to apply for rental assistance.

It took me two years to be able to pay back our air ticket money. My social worker helped me with food, clothes vouchers, money and she also helped me secure a one-bedroom disability housing that was a lot cheaper than the private rental ($150 per week). Now I was receiving $100 a fortnight in rental assistance as well as the $360 a fortnight on Newstart. I moved out of the private rental after two months. This meant I had to pay back the bond of $750 that the government had paid to the landlord on my behalf because I breached my lease agreement by moving out ten months early. I also had to find someone to move into the rental unit and pay the rent for me to avoid further fines for breaching my lease agreement. My social worker and ARA helped me with finding a young South Sudanese man to rent my unit a week before I moved out and I was very happy when the lease was transferred into his name two weeks after I had moved out.

The food I received from ARA and the Salvation Army was enough for me to live on until I started receiving my Disability Support Pension (DSP) in early 2006. Jane was also providing me with food in 2005 when she could. The money I received from Centrelink went into paying rent, the air ticket money and my bond fine. ARA, the Salvation Army and the Department for Child Protection (Families SA) helped me with paying my bills here and there until I started receiving DSP. A week after I moved into the disability housing, the social worker and the manager for the disability housing helped me to apply for public housing, which was more permanent and affordable. Six months after arriving in Australia, I started receiving DSP, which meant that I was now able to pay my rent and bills and buy food for myself. I was also able to pay off my bond and the air ticket money and also help my sister back home in Uganda financially.

At the same time, I was able to save some money for my driving lessons. I started to learn to drive in December

2006 with an instructor, which cost me over $4,000. I was not lucky enough to have someone from the community to help me with driving lessons before going to an instructor, which would have meant that I would not need as many lessons and therefore could pay less money to the accredited driving instructor. There were people in the community, including my sister's husband, who volunteered their time to teach new arrivals to drive before they went to an instructor, but they didn't do the same to me. I didn't receive this service because my community had turned their backs on me months earlier because of the disagreement my sister and I had.

Ten months after moving into the disability housing, Housing SA offered me a two-bedroom public housing unit which was a lot cheaper than the disability housing and it was a good unit too. I didn't receive rental assistance for the public housing because the rent was already subsidised.

During this period, things deteriorated between my sister and me to the extent that she would refuse to talk to me on the phone or to invite me to her house for dinners. She would host dinners in her house for visitors coming from Africa, for New Year's Eve and many other events but she did not invite me. I, however, kept going to her house when I could to wash her dishes and cook meals for her and her family while she was at work or studying. Slowly, bit by bit, my sister came around, we worked through our differences and we became best friends. Now we tell each other everything about each other's private lives. The turning point came when she found out from our brother in South Sudan that I was pregnant with my first daughter. I didn't tell her that I was pregnant but I instead told my brother and sister in Africa and that was how she found out. I could have refused to allow my sister back into my life and to be involved in the life of my daughter five years after she threw me out of her house because, by that time, I was already settled in Australia and I had paid all my debts, but I would never disown my sister because I believe that blood is thicker than water. I also remembered the words of her husband, who told me way back in Uganda that no matter what people do to me in life, I should never become like them. He told me never to stop doing good things to people, including those who treat me badly. So that was exactly what I did because to me, two wrongs cannot make a right. There were times after my first daughter was born when I asked for or needed my sister's help and she has been there for me ever since. I would not have been able to receive that help from her with my children if I had put my walls up to her.

During this time before my sister and I were reconciled, I became socially isolated. Some people in my community, including Jane, Jimmy and his sister Sandy (who I talk about more in Chapter 7), for a very short period had sacrificed their time to help me with my grocery shopping and taking me to appointments, then everyone disappeared except for Jimmy and Sandy and her family and I still don't know the reasons why those people disappeared. All I know is that after my sister threw me out of her house, people started spreading rumours about me, saying that I was a prostitute. They said that I left because my sister would not allow me to bring men into her house! Nobody said that my sister threw me out but that I had left. They said that I was going to end up on the streets because they thought that I would not be able to pay for my rent, bills and food, but I proved them wrong. They were shocked and embarrassed to find out that I was renting a two-bedroom house, I was working and studying at the same time and I continued to complete my government and community resettlement program, and I generally resettled in Australia successfully without the support of my community. After my sister threw me out of her house, some people refused to come to my house and others refused to let their children come to my house, saying that I was a bad influence. But by 2018, they were telling their children to call me aunty and saying that I am an inspiration and a good influence for the younger people in our community. From being a bad influence to a good influence and an inspiration!

If you are reading this book and you are going through or have gone through similar life experiences to mine, well here is the good news. God will always use a negative experience in your life to create something good or positive from it for his own Glory and that was what happened to me. God would never hurt us but He will allow things to happen in our lives to rearrange and shape our lives. For example, God allowed the coronavirus to shut the whole world down in 2020 in order to soften our hearts and to also help us rethink how we live and how we treat others in our families, communities, and our countries and in society.

Whenever I went to community gatherings between 2005 and 2013, people would refuse to shake hands with me and they would refuse to sit next to me. People would look at me in a bad way and others would point at me and laugh. I became a hot topic of gossip in my community but still I didn't give up. My own South Sudanese Equatorian community had become a very toxic environment for me to be in but I came back to the community. Whenever there was something happening in the community, someone would ring me and tell me about it but they would warn me not to mention it to anyone that they were the one who had invited me. This was meant to break me so I would isolate myself and suffer from lifelong mental health issues, but I refused to let the negativity and toxic environment break me. Instead I continued attending community events, including meetings, birthdays, Easter and Christmas celebrations, whenever I could and now,

I am glad to report that as I write, I am a valued member of my community. I also continued to attend funerals and to contribute financially to my community when I could.

I have recently been appointed a South Australian assistant state coordinator for the Federation of Equatoria Community Association in Australia (FECAA) and the National Secretary for the FECAA Women's Support Group. I am so honoured and humbled to be coordinating projects in my community in South Australia. All this has happened because I didn't give up. In June 2019, the same community and the same people who rejected me years earlier came together to celebrate my achievements during my book launch. The same people who didn't speak to me fifteen years ago are now ringing to check on me, to ask for help from me or just to chat. Some of those people are, however, still too ashamed to even talk to me. I have forgiven them and I hope that one day they can forgive themselves too.

After my sister threw me out, our family matter became a community and a public issue where people spread rumours about me and others exaggerated everything to make the situation look and sound bigger or worse than what it actually was. This impacted a lot on my relationship with my sister for a period of time. The people in my community who didn't have an issue sticking their noses into our family business are the same people who, when I finally started talking about it publicly and telling my side of the story, said it was a private family matter and that I should not be talking about it publicly!

While people were wasting time gossiping and spreading rumours about me, I was busy studying and working. By the time they had finished gossiping about me, I had completed my Social Work degree and I was graduating. Others later came to realise that what they were saying about me was not true and they came to apologise to me. A few months after my sister threw me out, a woman from my community who was one of the ringleaders in spreading the rumours bumped into me at the Women's and Children's Hospital in Adelaide. I was wearing an Interpreters ID badge around my neck as I had gone there to interpret for a woman in my own community who was pregnant. This lady was shocked and she bought lunch for me afterwards to apologise to me for the rumours. She asked me where I was living and who I was living with and I told her that I was renting a two-bedroom house and living alone. I also told her that I was studying a Social Work degree at the University of South Australia. She couldn't believe it because it was very hard at the time for refugee migrants to get admission into the university, and she wondered how I did it without any support from my community. She was also shocked and embarrassed because a large number of young and single South Sudanese people, even after ten years of being in Australia, were unable to afford to pay their own rent and live alone by themselves. Most of them live in shared accommodation to share the rent and the bills but there I was, less than a year in a new country, and I was living alone in a two-bedroom house, I was studying at the university and working as an interpreter at the same time.

At least I had Jimmy there to help me. Jimmy was the only person who didn't reject me and he remained my friend during that tough time but in 2015, he too rejected me big time after everything else had settled in my life (see Chapter 7).

Five

LESSONS LEARNT FROM MY RELATIONSHIP WITH EDDIE

Growing up with a disability in the South Sudanese community, I have encountered a great deal of relationship challenges, whether boyfriend relationships, family relationships or just any other everyday relationship or friendship. I have met many African friends in my lifetime but most of them took advantage of me and they left me hurt and disappointed. As if the hard life of being a refugee and having a disability was not enough, I experienced an unthinkable act of rape. In July 2002, I was raped by a South Sudanese man who went unpunished for what he did to me because others thought he did nothing wrong. Generally, South Sudanese men and most African men are believed to be 'right' all the time and that they don't do anything wrong or make mistakes. And that's why when a relationship is going well, the man will take all the credit, but if anything bad happens in that relationship, people will automatically conclude that it was the woman's fault. In cases of rape, the woman is always blamed for the rape, not the man. Because it is believed that men are visual creatures and that most men see women as sexual objects, people will say the woman might have dressed indecently or that the woman caused the rape because she was out alone at certain times of the day, at the man's house or in places where she shouldn't have been and that this led to the rape. In my own case, people said that if I didn't go to that man's house, that I would not have been raped! I'm not saying that women should walk naked but, women should feel free to dress in what feels appropriate to them and their body type and women should also be able to walk freely at any time without being judged or sexually assaulted. He was my best friend, I looked up to him and thought I could trust him, but he betrayed my trust and ruined our friendship.

Here in Australia, I have had three different and in-teresting relationships with three different men. Two of them were South Sudanese men and one was a Ugandan man. My first relationship was with the Ugandan man, Eddie, who was very charming. My relationship with him was somewhat none too romantic but fun. My second relationship was with Harry and this was more a story of a princess rescuing her prince, not the other way round, but there was no happy ending. A baby, however, came out of this relationship and that was a big blessing to me. My third relationship was with a handsome South Sudanese man, Jimmy, but this relationship was abusive mentally, emotionally and financially. We were married by tradition in May 2015 in South Australia and we moved in together nearly two years after we first started dating but he moved out ten months later and has never returned. Jimmy had never been married before. This was my first long-term romantic relationship and it involved the first part of traditional marriage rites (which I explain further in Chapter 7) but I felt very alone, unloved and the relationship with Jimmy didn't last. It ended unexpectedly a few years later. Two babies came out of this relationship. One of the babies is unfortunately growing up in heaven. I certainly learnt valuable lessons from my three relationships that I hope will help me a lot in making future relationship decisions.

Eddie was a very handsome, loving, charming and bubbly Ugandan Christian man who was full of life. He used to make me laugh a lot and he has so far been the only man who has really made me laugh. The only time I was sad and cried with Eddie was in 2008 after he was deported back to Uganda. I cried because I missed him. There was not a single dull or boring moment with Eddie in it. We were not in a real romantic relationship but we felt comfortable in each other's company. There were a few times when we kissed but we spent most of our time talking to each other about everything and anything. We enjoyed going for long drives together on Saturdays and we also watched movies together. Eddie was adventurous and full of life like me. He was also a good cook. So far, I have not met a man who doesn't know how to cook. All the three men I have had in my life were good cooks. We mostly talked about God, and we read the Bible together and we had Bible discussions between the two of us about the verses we had read. We set a task to each other to read a verse every day and then we would talk about the verses we had read during the week on Saturdays. We both found out that we like keeping a Bible in our cars and we helped each other to keep our faith strong. We mostly watched Christian movies and a few romantic movies together on Saturdays. We had a really good two-year relationship. He used to impersonate the Pastor's preaching and I thought it was hilarious. Every time he came to my house, he would stand at the corner and pretend to be Pastor so and so and he would preach with passion, sounding exactly like that Pastor and sweat would even be dripping from his face while he was preaching. I didn't need to listen to the radio or watch TV whenever he was preaching but just sit and watch him and laugh sometimes.

A few months into our relationship, we both realised that we were suited as friends but not as romantic lovers. I had just started my Social Work studies and I told him that I didn't want any serious relationship or anything that would interfere with my studies and he agreed. Eddie was a short man and I didn't find him attractive even though he was very good looking. I am attracted to tall and slim-built men with full, short beards. He accepted and respected my decision and we remained friends, though we both hoped that, with time, we would develop feelings for each other and hopefully get married and have children one day, but that was not meant to be.

Eddie was the man that gave me my first kiss and, boy, he was a very good kisser. Even though Eddie didn't have higher educational qualifications and even though he was working in a chicken factory at the time, he never had any issues hanging out with me and being in public with me like the other two men did. He wasn't ashamed of me and he was not ashamed to be around me or to be with me around other people. He took me to the Adelaide Hills in 2006 and we toured the hills together for the first time. On another occasion, in 2007, he took me to one of the German market events in the Adelaide Hills and we had lunch together. We went to community events together. He even accompanied me to a funeral gathering at my friend's house once. He had no issues driving me to the funeral and staying there with me, and he introduced himself to the mourners afterwards as my boyfriend. We went shopping together on so many occasions and he paid for the groceries. He also used to pick fresh roses from his garden to give to me every time he came to my house and he made me feel special. Eddie and I understood each other on every level.

He was always very proud and happy to introduce me to others as his girlfriend. I thought that Eddie was an angel sent to me by God to keep me out of trouble but I soon learnt that angels do not come in the form of men and Eddie was certainly no angel. He had his own weaknesses as a human which resulted in him being deported back to Uganda in mid-2008. I also soon learnt that he was a very controlling and very jealous man who could sometimes become possessive. If I went for two days without calling him, if he saw me talking to other men or if he came to my house and I didn't pay attention to him for some reason, he would become very angry and would throw things, smashing them on the floor, or he would just leave and drive away very erratically.

I remember one Thursday evening in 2007 when I was doing my assignment on my computer, he came to my house unannounced and demanded that I stop doing my assignment and attend to him immediately. I told him to make himself comfortable on the couch and that I would be with him shortly. I also told him that my assignment was due the following day and that I had to finish it. Ten minutes later, he got up, threw the DVDs he had brought with him on the floor and broke the covers and then he raced out of my house. I followed him into the car park and asked what was wrong but he yelled at me, saying that he had come all the way from his house to spend time with me when he should have been sleeping after work but all I did was ignore him. He said that I took my assignment to be more important than him. I tried to apologise but he told me that if he was to accept my apology, I should drive to his house and apologise to him there. He said that if I didn't go to his house and apologise, that he would never come to my house or speak to me ever again. He drove off at a very high speed and almost ran me over. I fell onto the ground and hurt my knee but he kept driving and did not stop to check if I was okay. I went back into my house, got my keys and handbag and I drove to his house, which was thirty minutes away. I expected to hear and see another explosion or meltdown but when I arrived at his house, he was completely different, the humble and sweet Eddie that I knew. The man who had been in my house a few minutes ago had disappeared. He quickly apologised and ended up cooking dinner for me. I left my assignment and went to his house because I didn't want to lose him and our friendship.

When I first met Eddie in mid-2006, I had no driver's licence and no car. I had not even started to learn to drive but Eddie drove me everywhere in his car during that time whenever he was free. Every time I wanted to go somewhere and he was available to drive me, I could ring him and he would come to my house without hesitation.

On every one of our long drives, he would ask me to pay him money for fuel and I was paying him up to $150 per trip sometimes. Because I wasn't driving at the time, I didn't know how much money was needed to fuel a small sedan so I gave him what I thought was reasonable. He never asked me to give him any amount, he only asked me to give him money to fill up his car and I always chose the amount to give him but he didn't give me back any change. Back then, a litre of fuel was 89 cents in Adelaide and I am sure that he would have used less than $50 to fuel his small car. Not until I started driving did I realise that he had duped me and taken advantage of me. I was always happy to go out on those long drives with him where we had lunches together and I thought that he was a gentleman who liked to spoil me, but I later learnt that I was the one funding all those trips the whole time without realising. I was new to Australia and I trusted him but he took advantage of my innocence.

This is a common practice in my community and in the African community in general where some people take advantage of new arrivals by spending their money or creating big bills in their names for them to pay. Another time when I was still new to the country, someone came to my house and made phone calls to Africa from my landline and I ended up paying a $400 telephone bill. I was, however, able to restrict the calls to local calls only and no calls to mobile phones from my landline after I had paid the bill. I also know of some people in the African community who were struggling to resettle in Australia because the friends who had proposed that they come to Australia and were already resettled here took car loans in their names when they had just arrived in the country, and those friends used the cars for their own personal and family commutes. These people also accumulated a lot of fines for their newly arrived friends to pay because they parked in no-parking zones, were caught speeding or ran red lights. Other resettled people would take out credit cards in the names of the new arrivals for their own use and yet the new arrivals were the ones who had to pay back the credit card debts.

In early 2008, Eddie started to ignore my calls sometimes and then make up stories later to make me believe that he was either in trouble, in the shower or that his phone was not charged or not working properly and that was why he didn't either see or hear his phone ringing. I soon found out that he was engaged to be married to another woman (a white woman) in four months' time. I failed to understand when he had met her, how long they had been seeing each other and how he had time to spend with her for them to be engaged as he was working Monday to Friday, 7am to 5pm, and he was with me every Saturday from 10am, and sometimes to 11pm or 12am. There were also times when he had slept in my house after falling asleep on the couch while watching TV or a movie. He was also with me every Sunday afternoon after Church. There was only one Saturday in early 2008 when he didn't come to my house because he had to work that day; that was what he told me. It turned out that on that same Saturday, he went to the beach with Susan and Mark, a friend of ours, and that was when he proposed to Susan with a ring that she had bought for him to propose with. Susan lived in the same apartment block as Eddie and her unit was above his. They met one Sunday morning in the car park when they were both going to Church (different churches), two weeks before they were engaged. Within the two weeks, Susan had moved in with Eddie and she had introduced him to her Pastor, who told her that something was not right with the relationship and that they should take it very slow, but Susan wouldn't listen. She had been praying for an African husband for many years and when she saw Eddie, she thought that God had answered her prayers so she quickly moved in with him before another woman did. Susan was also planning to move to another Church and marry Eddie at the beach since her Pastor was against their relationship.

Our friend Mark was also not comfortable with what was happening so he told Susan to talk to me and find out what kind of relationship Eddie and I had before she moved to another Church and married him. Mark and Susan went to the same Church. One Sunday afternoon after Church, Susan and Mark rang me and she asked if I was Eddie's sister, because that was what he had told her, but I told her that we were not related and that we were not from the same country. Eddie was from Uganda and I was from South Sudan. Susan asked where Eddie had been the day before, which was Saturday, and I told her that he had been with me and also the evening before that. She rang Eddie and asked if we were really related and he said no. He openly told her that I was his girlfriend and that he hoped to marry me one day in the future. Susan asked him what about her and he said that he wouldn't marry a woman that moved in with him two weeks after they had met. He said that he wasn't interested in their relationship and that was why he continued to spend time with me even after she had moved in with him. Susan asked Eddie to apologise for lying to her about me but he refused and she cried. I was on the phone and I heard everything. Instead, Eddie apologised to me on the phone for not telling me about Susan. He also came to my house straight away after the phone call to apologise to me in person. Strangely, Eddie didn't apologise to Susan or even acknowledge that he had hurt her. Instead, he blamed her for everything by saying that she was the one that forced him into the relationship. Eddie's relationship with Susan brought up a lot of complications and all the secrets that Eddie had been hiding about how he came to Australia were exposed and he was deported back to Uganda in 2008 as a result. He was not to return to Australia or go to any other Western countries for five years.

Eddie had enrolled himself in a Theology course in South Australia but he couldn't continue with his studies, even though he had paid for the course in full. Four years after he was deported, he tried to come back to Australia to complete his course but his application was rejected. He pleaded with me to give him a reference but things were out of my hands. He applied to go to America but his application was also rejected. As for Susan, I never heard from her again and I don't know what has happened to her. I was in a way relieved that Eddie was deported back to Uganda because I detest dishonest people who claim to be men of God.

Eddie and I met at Church. One Sunday afternoon in mid-2006, I was sitting in the Church during testimony time when the Pastor asked if there was anyone in the congregation who would like to give a testimony, and I saw this handsome, charming and good-looking man walk to the front of the Church and introduce himself to the congregation as 'Eddie' from Uganda. He thanked God for bringing him to Australia and for providing him with a job here. He also said that he was alone in Australia and that he would like to meet and get to know a few people from the Church that he could ring and talk to or visit sometimes. After the service, I waited at the door to greet him. Surely enough, he came out of the Church and I greeted him in Luganda, a language in Uganda.

We got talking and we straight away connected and we exchanged numbers. He rang me that Sunday evening and we spoke for more than two hours on the phone and that was how we became friends.

Eddie and I lost contact and I don't miss him anymore. My relationship with him has made me become a lot wiser. Now if someone invites me out to lunch or for a drive, I will ask that person first if I am going to pay for the food and fuel before I leave my house. Culturally, if an African man asks someone to go out to lunch or for a drive with him, he would pay for the food, drinks and the fuel but he would not ask the friend to do it. In addition, if an African woman invites people to her house for dinner, she would provide everything — the people she invited would just come and eat without contributing anything.

Six

LESSONS LEARNT FROM MY RELATIONSHIP WITH HARRY

Harry was a tall, handsome and slim-built South Sudanese man with a lot of facial hair. Physically, he was exactly the kind of man I would fall for but he was carrying a lot of baggage on his shoulders, including poverty, home-lessness, alcohol abuse and mental health issues, which wasn't what I needed. I had just come out of a hard life in refugee camps in Uganda and I equally experienced a lot of challenges in my first two years of being in Australia from 2005 to 2007. When I met Harry, I had paid all the bond and the air ticket money (please refer to Chapter 4) and I had just started to feel like I was on the right track to getting resettled in Australia.

In mid-2008, I met a lady from my community at a doctor's waiting room. We got talking and she told me what was happening in the community. She said that a man called 'Harry' was struggling to settle in Australia and that he had resorted to drinking a lot of alcohol and that he had become homeless as a result. Harry was an Evangelist and he had helped a lot of people financially, including new arrivals in the South Sudanese community in South Australia. He was working and studying but he lost his job and eventually stopped studying shortly after his long-term relationship ended suddenly. I didn't know Harry that well personally before I met this lady. I had seen him at community events months earlier and we said hello to each other but we never talked. The lady said that Harry needed help but the community had turned their backs on him. She wanted to help him but she was afraid that she would get into trouble with her husband if he found out. I asked her if she had Harry's number and she said that she would get it for me. A few months later in early 2009, the lady rang me and she gave me Harry's number. I rang Harry and we spoke a little bit on the phone. He didn't sound well and I asked to meet him in person and he agreed to meet me at my house. A week later, he came to my house and we talked. He appeared weak, tired, hungry and drowsy. His body was swollen, and his face, arms and feet appeared to be filled with fluid.

When he came to my house, he had not eaten proper food for weeks and I suggested that he go to see a doctor and a psychologist. He was open to seeking professional help and I also offered to help him with what I could.

When he came to my house, he hardly had any clothes on and he was sleeping in the park toilets in the city at the time. I asked him to come and stay in my spare bedroom while I helped him look for alternative accommodation and he agreed. I later helped him to apply for public housing but he didn't end up securing accommodation because he had a bad tenancy record. I am glad that God enabled me to provide Harry with shelter, food and clothing when everybody in the community had turned their backs on him.

I took him to Vinnie's shop in Norwood to buy decent clothes and I also took him to the barber shop for his hair and beard to be shaved. I then took him back home to my house and he had a good and proper hot shower for the first time in months. He had dinner and a good sleep in my spare bedroom. Two weeks later after receiving medical treatment, he was looking good and I asked him if he would like to go to South Sudan to meet his parents and come back to Australia with blessings from his parents. He had been separated from his parents for twenty-four years. When he was eleven years old, he was abducted from his aunt's house by the Sudanese People's Liberation Army (SPLA) and he was forced to train as a child soldier. He never returned home to his parents but he was lucky to find his way to Australia via Kakuma refugee camp in Kenya. He agreed and we went to book his return air ticket, which I paid for. That afternoon, he was filled with joy and emotions and he forced me into sleeping with him. He said that sleeping with me was the only thing he could offer me to thank me for everything I had done for him. After he realised what he had done, he tried to run. But I stopped him. I told him that it was okay and that I was not going to report him to the police. He stayed and the rest is history.

The time came in October 2009 and he went to Africa. His father, mother and close relatives rang me and they all gave me their blessings for sending him back to them alive after nearly twenty-five years of not seeing him. Harry, though, didn't want to marry me because, to him, marrying a woman with a disability was a taboo. He instead married another woman in South Sudan before he returned to Australia in January 2010. He used the pocket money I gave him to buy an engagement ring for the woman in Africa and he also hosted a very big engagement party using my hard-earned money. I was working with Human Services (formerly known as Disability SA) at the time and I was able to save that money. Initially my plan was to save some money towards a mortgage but I soon realised that helping Harry was a huge financial setback for me because by the time he left my house in January 2010, I had already spent over $10,000 on him. And that was on top of the money he took from my wallet without my permission and minus all the other hidden expenses, including food, clothes, transport, electricity, internet, telephone and water.

I was angry, hurt and disappointed with his level of disrespect towards me and my belongings. Four days after he returned from South Sudan, he moved out into emergency housing with a few of his belongings as a way of speeding up his public housing application. I went to work that morning when he was sleeping and when I came back home, he was gone without leaving me a note. I rang him to ask where he was and he said that he was in emergency housing because he wanted to move out into his own house and be independent again. By this time, he was already planning to get a job and then bring the woman from Africa but, for some reason, the woman is still in Africa as I write now. He said that I had done enough in helping him and that he didn't think it was necessary to talk to me about his future plans. I asked him what had happened in Africa as he had been quiet and withdrawn since he returned but he terminated the call. I was shocked because he had changed!

A week after he moved out, in February 2010, he came back to my house sick and I nurtured him. He was there for two days and things happened and that was when I became pregnant with my first daughter. When I told him in March that I was pregnant with his child, he refused to be involved. Instead, he told me to do whatever I wanted to do with the pregnancy. He said that if I wanted to keep the pregnancy, let the baby be my gift to pay for everything I had done for him. He also said that he did not want people to know that I had a child with him and that he did not want my baby to know that he was her biological father. I ignored everything he said and invited him to come to the hospital with me for my first antenatal appointment but he refused. He even refused to sign any paperwork to do with my daughter, including her birth certificate. After my daughter was born, I tried to involve him in her life but he refused. A week after she was born, he came to the hospital at night very drunk. He could barely stand on his feet and he was making noise. I asked him to leave and come back in the morning when he was sober so we could talk but he didn't come back.

On my daughter's third birthday I invited him and he came to record a video of the birthday party to show his father that he was the one who had organised the party, and invited and fed everyone in the video. He left after he had finished recording the video and still didn't want to be involved. When I was working an hour's drive away from home in 2013, I asked him to look after my daughter since he was not working to avoid me paying extra money to childcare. I was always arriving back home from work after the childcare centre had closed or was just about to close and my daughter was always the last one left at childcare, but he asked me to pay him for looking after his own daughter and I did! He looked after her for two weeks and I paid him a sum of $250, which was way more than the money I pay the childcare centre. I was paying the childcare centre $92 a week. He was eating my food, using my electricity and using my house phone and internet during the day when I was at work but I still paid him money to look after his own daughter and I didn't complain because I wanted him to have a relationship with her. I later realised that paying him to have a relationship with my daughter was not worth it. I should not have been paying him to have a relationship with his own daughter but he should be responsible and look after our daughter. He came back on the third week to apologise and to look after my daughter again but without pay this time and I agreed. But two days later, he disappeared, leaving my daughter in the carport on a freezing winter evening! He took whatever little money I had in the house and he went to Africa, leaving my daughter with no shoes or socks and no jacket on. He had rung me a few minutes earlier and told me that he had to go because there was an emergency where he was living and I told him that I was five minutes away and that I would be home soon, but he left before I arrived. I came back from work and found my daughter in the cold in the carport crying and shivering terribly. That night, she came down with a fever, cough and runny nose.

When Harry was living in my house in 2009, he treated my rental property like his own and he almost got me evicted from that house. One day I came back home from work to find that he had moved all his belongings from a commercial storage unit to my house without my consent. He packed some things of mine away to make space for his own things without my permission. He also brought his homeless friends from the city parklands to my house on a regular basis during the day when I was at work and they ate, drank alcohol and played music very loud every time, which made the neighbours complain to the Public Housing Authority. Sometimes they fought and bottles and glasses were smashed on the floor but he always cleaned the house before I came back to get rid of the evidence. He used the money he took from my wallet to buy alcohol for his friends and they consumed all my food in the fridge and in the pantry.

By this time, he was pretending to me that he was volunteering in the city and also looking for work so he got up very early in the morning every day and got himself ready to leave the house before I did. I later found out that he went to sit at the bus stop until I left for work and then he would return home to sleep or to entertain his friends. I was giving him transport money every morning thinking that he was volunteering and looking for work at the same time but he wasn't. I took my keys off him after I found out that he had been lying to me and I threatened to cancel his flight but he pleaded with me not to cancel his flight. He said that if he didn't go to South Sudan to see his parents, then my hard work of getting him back on his feet and making him a better person again in the last few months was for nothing. Even though I knew that he was manipulating me, I did not cancel his flight. Instead, I put myself in his shoes and I allowed him to go to Africa. He promised me that he would do the right thing and make me proud but he didn't. I later discovered that he had cut many copies of the keys to my house and I was scared that he might have given keys to his friends so I installed a chain lock on the front door from the inside. I used the back door as he didn't have a key to the back door and only after I had not seen him for six months after he had moved out did I start using the front door again, once I was sure he was completely gone. By this time, I was heavily pregnant.

It took me seven whole months of pleading with him for him to come and collect the rest of his things from my spare bedroom. I told him that I needed that room for my baby and he finally came with his friend to collect his things. His friend was surprised to see that I was pregnant and he rang me after they had collected Harry's things from my house. He asked me where the father of my unborn baby was and I told him that Harry was the father but he didn't believe me. He said that there was no way Harry could be the father of my unborn baby. He was surprised that his best friend would not mention to him that I was pregnant with his first child. He said that Harry had always been saying that he wanted to have children and now that he had got one on the way, he was not talking about it! I told him that Harry did not want to have a child with a woman with a disability. His friend was shocked and angry. He said that if I had told him that Harry was the father of my unborn baby before they came to my house, he would have talked some sense into his head and they would not have collected his things. Instead, he would have forced Harry to stay with me, help me and look after me and my baby. He tried to talk to Harry but Harry still denied being the father of my daughter. Now that my daughter is older, he is starting to tell people that I refused to allow him to have access to his daughter.

In mid-2016 after Jimmy had left (which you will read about in Chapter 7), Harry sent a lady from his Church to come and check if I needed help with anything. The lady said that Harry was working and that he was available to transport my daughter to and from school for as long as I allowed him to. Because I was not allowed to drive at the time for six weeks due to my caesarean wound, I gave Harry another chance to build a relationship with his daughter by transporting her to and from school. I thought that he really wanted to be involved in her life this time but this assistance would soon come to an end. He dropped her to and from school for three weeks and then he went to Africa a week before the end of the school term. When he returned in February 2017, my daughters and I had already moved to a new house and he tried to contact me but I told him that he was no longer welcome in my house or in my daughter's life. He didn't show any love, responsibility and commitment to my daughter and he was messing with her emotions. He was telling my daughter things that he knew nothing about and things that were not true. For example, he told her that when she was born, she was so tiny and that she cried a lot but he held her on his chest to make her go to sleep and that she would sleep for a long time. He told her that she always fell asleep every time he held her, which was not true. My daughter was big when she was born and Harry never held her.

He was also making big promises that he couldn't afford or keep. He told my daughter in the car so many times that he had a big house in South Sudan that was more beautiful than the house we lived in and that she was going to inherit that house in South Sudan one day. He also said that when my daughter was older, he would open a big hotel in South Sudan and would name it after her. He was saying to my daughter things like, you don't have to be a graduate to be rich. Since he came to Australia twenty years earlier, he had been living in shared accommodation. He could not even afford to pay his own rent and yet he was telling my daughter that he would open a big hotel for her.

Within two weeks of him having access to my daughter, her behaviour changed. She wasn't that keen about going to school anymore. On one occasion, she took another child's lunchbox and ate that child's lunch, claiming that her own lunch was not good because it didn't have a chocolate bar in it. I had found out a few days earlier that Harry was telling my daughter not to eat the lunch I prepared for her unless there was a chocolate bar, energy drink, cake or other sweet things in her lunchbox. I also found out that he had been packing chocolate bars, cakes and sweets for her to eat at school every day. On two occasions, he asked my daughter to order food from the school canteen for lunch because he didn't pack lunch for her on those two days. I found this out after the school sent the two invoices for me to pay. I went to school, paid the money and I stopped them from giving food to my daughter. Every day, my daughter returned home with her lunchbox full and untouched and I didn't know why until I found out that he was also packing a lunchbox for her with lots of sugary stuff in it. Harry came into my daughter's life with a mission to destroy her life and to destroy my relationship with her. All of a sudden, my daughter refused to eat her healthy lunch that did not have chocolates, cakes or sweets with it. He had unravelled my five years of work raising my daughter to be a healthy child in one week. It took me months to get my daughter back on track and living the healthy kind of life that she was used to.

Harry has not seen or spoken to her since 2016. He has, however, been telling people in the community that I refused to have a relationship with him because he is not educated like me and that I have not allowed him to see my daughter because he is poor, which is not true. When I met Harry and offered him help, and when I became pregnant with his first child, I was already educated more than him. I don't know what he meant by saying all the things he said in our community. Harry is not paying child support not because he is poor but because he refused to. He threatened to hurt me and my daughter weeks before she was born if I told the government that he was the biological father.

Like Jimmy, Harry was ashamed of me because of my disability so he refused to go anywhere with me. Every time we went to the shops, we would use two trolleys for our groceries and we wouldn't see each other until we finished shopping. After he finished shopping, he would wait for me at the checkout area for me to pay for the things he had collected and then he would leave and wait for me again in the carpark for me to drive him home. He had lost his driver's licence to drink driving years earlier. One day we bumped into someone he knew at the checkout area and the lady congratulated him for having a beautiful young girlfriend but he told the woman that I was his sister and that I was too young to be his girlfriend. Harry was seven years older than me but his lifestyle made him look way older. If he had money, I'm sure he would not have gone to the shops with me. He also refused to sit down and have a meal together with me in the house because to him, having a meal with a woman with a disability is a taboo but he was happy to take my money and he was also happy to sleep with me! Whenever I was cooking and he saw that dinner was almost ready, he would find a reason to leave the house or he would simply leave the house without telling me when I wasn't looking and then he would return at 11pm when I was asleep and eat then. There were times when he left his key in the house and he would wake me up to open the door for him when I had just gone to sleep. He also used to wake up every morning at 3am or 4am to eat so we wouldn't have to eat breakfast together especially on weekends and on public holidays.

There were times when he went to buy cooked food with my money and he ate it in the house alone without giving any to me. He often did that if I came back from work late and when dinner was late. He had to eat dinner at 6pm but without me, not a minute earlier or later. If he wanted something from me like big money that was more than $100 or if he wanted sex and I wasn't giving it to him, he would cook very yummy food and he would clean the house that day before I returned from work. When I arrived home, he would be waiting for me at the door to hug me, take my keys and handbag, then he would make for me a beautiful cup of tea before serving me dinner. As soon as he got what he wanted, he would disappear for weeks and would only return for more money when the money was finished. I fell for his tricks for a short period of time but I soon realised that he was playing me so I stopped giving him anything and that was when he started to bring his homeless friends into my house. It's sad when you help someone but they don't appreciate it, I said to myself. Instead, they will take your kindness for granted. I believe that my kind heart has drawn me closer to the wrong people but I have learnt a lesson from my relationship with Harry. Next time, I will be careful not to take people into my house or into my life when helping them.

Seven

LESSONS LEARNT FROM MY RELATIONSHIP WITH JIMMY

Marriage and disability in the South Sudanese culture is a very big issue. To the best of my knowledge, there are not many young men in the South Sudanese community who have married or are prepared to marry women with disabilities as their first wives, but Jimmy did. Because the culture allows polygamous marriages, if a South Sudanese woman with a disability is to be married, she would only be married to an older South Sudanese man as a second, third or even fourth wife. These may be South Sudanese men who already have older children from previous marriages or whose previous relationships have failed, or they may be men with a range of social and mental health issues, including alcohol addiction and poverty. Other South Sudanese men, in Australia especially, are willing to lay with a woman with a disability and even have children with her but they would not take responsibility for their children and they would not want to be seen in public or identified with those women with disabilities. Others do not want to be known as the fathers of the children with mothers with disabilities. They would sneak into those women's houses in the middle of the night, sleep with them and then leave at dawn before the neighbours are awake. As I described in the last chapter, the biological father of my first daughter told me after he found out that I was pregnant with his first child not to tell anyone in the community that he was the father. He told me that he did not want people to know that he had had a child with a woman with a disability.

Since I was young, I have always prayed to have a husband, have children, have many grandchildren, have a big extended family and build a clan of my own but, unfortunately, in part, that has not happened yet. I have, however, not lost hope of walking down the aisle one day. I still think that my husband is out there somewhere and that he will soon reveal himself.

Jimmy is a tall, handsome, slim-built and quiet man who loves to help others. He is a South Sudanese man but he has always identified and introduced himself to others as a Ugandan man. He was exactly the kind of man I could hold close to my heart for the rest of my life but my relationship with him didn't last until death do us part as I had hoped. We lost our middle daughter to stillbirth and things started to go downhill from there, and then he left two weeks after our third daughter was born. We also experienced a great deal of external negative energy, which resulted in our marriage breakdown. I have learnt from this time never to let anyone come in between me and my partner in the future, no matter who and no matter what.

Jimmy and I first met in my sister's house in 2005 on the first day I arrived in Australia. Three months later, after I had moved into the disability housing mentioned in Chapter 4, Jimmy started coming to my house to put my rubbish bins out on the street the night before the rubbish collection day and to also bring the bins back in after they had been emptied. He also brought filtered drinking water for me on a regular basis and he took me to the shops to show me where to buy groceries and African food. Since I came to Australia, I don't drink unfiltered water because it makes me develop sinus issues. When I first met Jimmy, I didn't know that he was interested in me romantically. All I knew was that he was a good friend. He didn't say anything or indicate to me that he was interested in me romantically and I also didn't pick up on any sign from him that he was interested, so I treated him like a friend but all that changed in 2014 after we started dating.

It all started with a phone call one evening in October 2013 when Jimmy asked to meet with me and talk about something very important. We couldn't talk for long on the phone then because I was driving, going to his sister Sandy's house with my daughter in the car. Even though I did pull over on the side of the road to talk to Jimmy when he rang, he decided that sitting in the car was not the right place to tell me what he wanted to talk to me about. Instead, he asked to meet with me somewhere in the next few days to talk. Sandy had always been nice to me since I came to Australia. On this particular day, she was overly friendly and she made a lot of good comments about me being a good mother, a strong and driven woman, an example to other women, and so on. The following day, Jimmy rang again and we spoke a little bit on the phone and then we met in my house a few days later.

During our conversation, he told me that he was interested in me romantically, that he wanted to settle down with me, and that he wanted me to be the mother of his children. Jimmy told me that he had been interested in me since the first day he saw me in my sister's house but that I wasn't paying attention to him. I was shocked and I hesitated because I had always looked up to him as a brother and as a friend, and also my daughter was two years old, turning three. I didn't want to have any form of a romantic relationship with any man when my daughter was still that young and I didn't want anything or anyone to jeopardise my relationship with her. I feared that any man I would have a relationship with would not treat my daughter well, so I planned to stay single until my daughter was at least sixteen years old and then I could start dating again. I raised the issue of my daughter being too young and my fears around that with Jimmy but he said that it was not a problem. He told me that he loved children and he reassured me that he would love and treat my daughter like his own.

I refused and what followed was that his two sisters (Sandy and Helen) came to my house all the time to visit me and to help me with even little things that I didn't need help with. For example, they would sometimes come to my house with cooked food and they would help me with doing my dishes, feeding my daughter, bathing her and putting her to bed, serving me food and putting the plates away after I had finished eating, sweeping and mopping my house on a regular basis as well as folding and putting my clothes away nicely. I wasn't allowed to touch anything whenever they were in my house and they pampered me and treated me like I was a princess and it felt so good. I wish things had continued that way. They had become regular visitors in my house even without invitation. Jimmy's sisters, Sandy especially, started to persuade me and she convinced me into accepting her brother's proposal. She told me that her brother had good intentions for me and she spoke very highly of him. She also said that they would all look after me and my daughter if I agreed to marry her brother. Because they had been so nice to me, and also because I had known Jimmy for such a long time, I accepted to have a relationship with him five months after he first contacted me, and we started seeing each other.

This is a common practice in the South Sudanese community where parents or relatives find husbands or wives for their single relatives. Even as I write now, there are still match-making relationships and arranged marriages happening in the South Sudanese community all over the world, including in South Sudan and in the refugee camps. Usually when this kind of marriage happens, people find themselves marrying strangers and people they don't love, and in most cases these marriages do not last. Even though Jimmy and I knew each other before the match making, our relationship didn't last because we were not on the same page, relationship wise. I was living in a small two-bedroom public housing with my daughter at the time. Jimmy's relatives even helped me a lot with promoting my campaign during the 2014 South Australian state election and handing out how to vote cards for me.

A few months into our relationship in 2014, Jimmy offered to look after my daughter one day when I was at university attending lectures and they both had a lot of fun together that day. He told me that there was no need for me to take my daughter to childcare when he was there doing nothing. And that was when I started to gain more trust in him because he took very good care of my daughter that day. When Jimmy and I first started dating, he was not working or studying so he had a lot of time to look after my daughter. In August 2014, he enrolled in a course at the Technical and Further Education College (TAFE) in Adelaide which enabled him to secure a job.

By late 2014, my daughter had already bonded with him and she had started to call him dad. I thought Jimmy had very good father qualities that I admired and he was a very good father figure to my daughter. I couldn't be happier. I thought that I had hit the jackpot but things would soon change for the worse. He and my daughter started to spend a lot of time together, and they went to the park and shopping together more often. I had also bonded with him because we were spending a lot of time together, especially on the weekends, though with less talking, but Jimmy would always find a way to shut me out of his life. He never discussed with me anything about himself, his family, his childhood, his job or just normal, everyday life things. I was always the one initiating everything in our relationship, including conversations and intimacy. Basically, I was the one running the relationship to make everything work and if I pulled back, the relationship would crumble.

Yet I was not the person wearing the pants in our relationship. In other words, I was not the person making the final decisions, and neither was he. His sister Sandy was our decision-maker. I was only there to make plans, make suggestions, bring issues to the table and come up with ideas, then he would take that information to his relatives to seek a second opinion and Sandy would then make the final decision in regards to how our relationship should be run and what should happen. If I agreed with Sandy's decisions, we would have no problems but if I disagreed with or opposed her decisions, Jimmy and I would have a lot of issues which, in most cases, would result in him moving out of our bedroom to the spare bedroom to sleep there for days or even weeks. Sandy took care of Jimmy after their mother passed away and he has always looked up to her as a mother figure and he felt happy to do anything in his life with her approval. There were also times when he had fallen asleep on the couch after watching TV to 2am or even 4am in the morning. He often did that if he was not going to work or helping his friends the following day so he could spend the whole day in bed sleeping to avoid spending time with me and talking to me. Every time I tried to talk to him about things, he would keep quiet and then I would hear about those same things I tried to talk to him about from Sandy. I was always hearing things from Sandy about Jimmy's childhood and their family, and I wondered why Sandy was the person to talk to me about those things and not Jimmy.

I accommodated his relatives' decisions for a little

while but I eventually became exhausted of being pushed around, so I started to make the decisions in our relationship by myself from late 2015 onwards. I still had to consult with Jimmy first, but this time I didn't wait for Sandy to make the final decision after consulting with him. I just went ahead and did what needed to be done without involving his sisters. I thought that I was doing the right thing by finally making the decisions in our relationship but, as you will soon find out, my not involving Sandy in the decision-making process in my relationship with her brother would soon come back to bite me. It didn't take long until my relationship with Jimmy started to fall apart. This relationship has taught me a lesson and next time, I will not fall for match-making relationships and I will not have a relationship with a man who needs approval from someone else before he can make a decision.

That was when I started to ask myself questions. Why is my relationship different from other women's relationships? Why are things different in my own relationship compared to others? What am I doing wrong that is making my relationship fall apart? I asked him on a number of occasions to tell me if I was doing things the wrong way, if I was crossing boundaries or if he felt that I was not including him in anything but he always told me that I was doing great. I told him from the beginning of our relationship that ever since I was a little girl in the refugee camps, I have always looked after myself, I have always managed every aspect of my life and that I have never really relied on anybody for anything. I told him to always let me know if he felt that I was not involving him enough in anything in our relationship, as a way of getting him to talk to me, but he insisted that I was doing great. So if I was doing great, I asked myself, why was my relationship falling apart? I was hurt and confused because he was giving me these mixed messages where one minute I was his sweet honey, the next minute I was his very sour lemon.

I later worked out that Jimmy and his relatives felt threatened by my education and they thought that I would be controlling him and pushing him into a corner. And that's why his relatives felt the need to intervene and try to control me from the get go before I had the opportunity to control him, but it was clear that they overstepped their boundaries. They didn't take time to get to know me well as a person but they instead made assumptions about me, and they judged me based on my education and achievements. In part, they were jealous of my achievements so they tried very hard to pull me down and to destroy my life by frustrating me and by making me feel worthless. They constantly called me a bad woman and made me feel like I was the bad person in the relationship. There were also times when Jimmy called me a bad mother in front of my daughter for no reason but just as a way of degrading me in her presence.

By calling me a bad woman or a bad mother, they were trying to mould me into the kind of wife they wanted for Jimmy and into the kind of mother they wanted for my daughter. I had tried to change myself in order to fit into their family dynamic but I later realised that I didn't need to change for anybody. To them, Jimmy was an angel or some kind of a god and I should bow down and worship him, but every time they tried to push me into a box, I came out the other side even stronger and they didn't like that.

In early February 2015, I found out that I was pregnant with my second child, Jimmy's first child, and he was very happy when I told him about it. Three months into my pregnancy, he started giving me $200 a month for food, but he stopped giving me money two months later, after we lost our baby. I used to think that Jimmy was not giving me money for groceries because we were not living together but even after we moved in together, he continued to not give me money and he never used his own money to do our grocery shopping. I had always given him money for our groceries and he saw nothing wrong with that. Every time I asked him why he did not use his money to do our grocery shopping, he would say that my money and everything that I had belonged to him and that there was nothing wrong in him using money from my account for our groceries. I also asked him why he didn't talk to me about his finances and why we didn't have a joint account and he said that he didn't know that he was supposed to share his finances with me! A few times, I went to the shops with him but before we left home, he would hide his wallet and bank cards somewhere in the house or in his car so that he wouldn't have to contribute money towards our groceries. If I ran out of money at the shops, he would say that he could not help me because he forgot his wallet at home and then we would have to put back some of the groceries as we were not able to pay for all of them on the day. We lived two minutes away, just behind the shopping centre, but still he could not go back home to get his wallet so we could pay for all the groceries we needed for that day.

Jimmy had never given me any money or bought me anything before I became pregnant with his first child. Since I became pregnant, he has always given me Christmas and birthday presents; even four years after he moved out of our family home, he has continued to give me presents. I don't know if he is giving me presents because he still has feelings for me or if he is just doing it to please our children. I like the presents but it would have been even better if he was giving me those when we were living together. In 2019 and 2020 he also gave me Mother's Day gifts, but I have now stopped him from giving me any more presents. He had never even taken me out for shopping or spoiled me like other men would, especially after finding out that I was pregnant with his first child. Jimmy didn't even take me out to dinner or on dates for the whole time we were seeing each other and when we were living together. It was always to events, and to dinners that I had been invited to, to birthday lunches and to movies I had organised as well as to weekends away that my friends had organised and paid for me that he came with me. Every time he received an invitation to birthday parties, graduation ceremonies, dinners or other events, including work events, he would go alone without me. Sometimes he would even go to the events without telling me and I would get to hear about it when the event was finished. If he was working that day, he would cancel going to that particular party or event. Sometimes he would cancel his shifts so he could attend events that he was invited to. He couldn't even ask me to go to the event on his behalf and represent him or represent us.

There were times when he cancelled doing things with me that we had planned to do together days, weeks or even months earlier just so he could spend time with his friends or help his friends or ex-girlfriends, Jasmine and Zara, without my knowledge. On many occasions, he went to teach Jasmine and Zara how to drive a car and then he would end up eating dinner at their houses. He was particularly spending a lot of time with Jasmine by helping her to complete and submit her online job applications, and he was also taking her to attend job interviews more than once a week. Jasmine was ringing and texting Jimmy at all hours of the night. I didn't believe that his relationship with Jasmine had really ended. I thought that this relationship was very much alive. He also helped Jasmine and Zara with moving houses and just transporting them to and from their personal appointments when he and I were supposed to do our own things together as a couple!

On another occasion, he went to the hospital to visit Zara's sister, who lost a baby to stillbirth in the same room that we had lost our baby in (which I talk more about in Chapter 15). He came back home stressed, restless and agitated. I asked him what the problem was and he told me that he went to the hospital with Zara to visit her sister and he was disturbed to find her in the same room that we lost our baby in. If he had not been back to that same hospital room where we lost our baby, I don't think he would have told me that he was with his ex-girlfriend Zara that day. This is a common practice by many African men where they choose to spend time with friends and other women instead of their wives and children. Also, in some Churches, African men sit on one side of the Church and women sit on the other side. At community gatherings South Sudanese men do not sit with their wives. They go together to the event or Church, but they don't sit together.

I was always left waiting and wondering about what he might be up to if he was not at home, who he was with, where he was and if he was safe. He made me feel as though his friends were more important than me and his friendships were far more important than my relationship with him. I used to and I still think that Jimmy is ashamed of me because I have a disability and that's why he never took me anywhere or to any events he had been invited to. He was happy to spend time with his ex-girlfriends and even take them to places but he never took me anywhere. I was always the one taking him to places and he saw nothing wrong with that. However, if I took him to events, he would introduce himself to others as my support worker, not as my partner or boyfriend, even at events where he should have been proud of me, such as when I received an award for my political work. This reflected badly on me because people thought I was having a sexual relationship with my support worker, which made me feel embarrassed and I fear it has meant that some people and some organisations have lost trust in me.

In early May 2015, Jimmy came home for a formal introduction where part of our traditional marriage rites were performed. In the South Sudanese Kuku culture, if a man loves a woman and that woman becomes pregnant before he has formally met the woman's parents and relatives, he has to make quick arrangements for the traditional marriage rites to be performed. But only part of the traditional marriage rites can be performed where dowry is not paid. After the baby is born, then all parts of the traditional marriage including dowry are completed. In the Western world, if a South Sudanese man loves a woman and he is committed to the relationship, he would propose with a ring to marry the woman during the formal traditional introduction ceremony. And then when all parts of the traditional marriage have been performed after the baby is born, they would get married in the Church. Others would still choose to get married before their baby is born. The way my relationship was going with Jimmy at the beginning, I was so confident that he was going to propose with a ring to marry me during our traditional marriage introduction ceremony but he didn't. I had even mentioned it to my best friend that I thought he was going to propose to me because I thought that he loved me enough to marry me. I didn't know that he only wanted me to be the mother of his children and nothing more. Because of how happy he was after he found out that I was pregnant with his first child, I thought that he was going to propose with a ring. I was disappointed, embarrassed, stressed and I began to panic when he didn't propose. My body was shaking because I knew then that he was not going to marry me, but at least he declared his love for me in front of family and friends. My hands were sweaty and I had to excuse myself from the ceremony to go to the toilet a few times and then I went to my room to cry and to calm myself down.

The stress and anxiety made me bleed even more. I had started bleeding weeks earlier but it was just spotting here and here and nothing serious (please refer to Chapter 15). That night of my traditional introduction ceremony, I bled a lot but the bleeding stopped in the early hours of the morning after I had calmed myself down. I didn't go to the hospital that night because the doctors at the Women's and Children's Hospital in Adelaide had told me weeks earlier when I had just started bleeding that if I didn't have tummy cramps and blood clots, I should not panic but I should still check in with them if the bleeding increased. I did ring them that night after everyone from the ceremony had gone and I completed a medical assessment on the phone where the midwife told me not to panic but to go to the hospital if the bleeding continued and if I felt any pain in my belly.

What I didn't know was that Jimmy was going to leave as soon as his child was born. I thought that he was not going to marry me but that he would still live with us. But I wasn't going to give up. I was going to fight for my relationship. Our traditional marriage was not completed because I was pregnant. In the South Sudanese Kuku culture, people don't talk about marriage or dowry when the woman is pregnant. They only complete the formal introduction ceremony where the man introduces himself as the father of the unborn baby and then they wait until the baby is born. If the woman becomes pregnant when she is still living with her parents, she has to go to the father of her baby's house and stay there until the baby is born. Once the baby is born, then the relatives and the elders of the community would sit down and talk about the future of the baby and the baby's parents.

As soon as the first part of our traditional marriage ceremony was completed, Jimmy became my daughter's father. Traditionally if a South Sudanese man marries a woman who already has a child or children from a previous relationship, and he completes a specific part of the traditional marriage rites to welcome those children into his family, which Jimmy did, he automatically becomes their father. We don't have the words stepfather, stepmother or step-siblings in our Kuku language so the 'stepfather' is automatically the father of the child/children born from a previous relationship. Likewise, if a man marries a woman when he already has children from a previous relationship, that woman would automatically become the mother of his children but she would not be referred to as a 'stepmother'. If the biological father of the child for some reason later turns up and wants his child/children back and the 'stepfather' is okay with that, he would then pay the 'stepfather' money or livestock, like cows or goats, to pay for the time and resources the 'stepfather' used in bringing up that child.

I don't believe that Jimmy has ever really loved me. I believe that he was pushed by his relatives to have a relationship with me and he did it to please them. Or rather he was pushed by someone who hates my guts into having a relationship with me to bring me down. My relationship with Jimmy was meant to destroy my life but God rescued me and He protected me and spared my life for a reason: to enable me to raise awareness about domestic violence in the South Sudanese community. The way Jimmy treated me did not reflect a man in love. The kind of love Jimmy gave me was a conditional love which was solely based on my relationship with his relatives and how well I related to them. For me to have Jimmy in my life, I had to be friends with his relatives and had to get along with everyone in his family. It felt like he didn't marry me for him but he married me for his relatives, which is a common practice by South Sudanese men. Most men in the South Sudanese community marry women to look after their ageing parents, relatives and the entire extended family where the woman will cook for them, clean after them, and wash and iron everyone's clothes. Instead of Jimmy sticking by me, his wife, in all circumstances and getting his relatives to come on board and agree to disagree with us, he gave me a condition to either agree with his relatives or to not have him in my life. He was always up there and I was down here and for me to come to his level, I had to work very hard to earn his love by pleasing his relatives. He never loved me for who I am but him and his relatives have always loved me for what

I am. Nothing I did to Jimmy was ever good enough, because I wasn't getting along with all his relatives and because I was not making them happy. His relatives' love for me was also based on how well my relationship with him was going. If Jimmy and I were talking, his relatives would also talk to me, they would be kind to me and they would also show me love, but if Jimmy and I were not talking, they would not talk to me. However, if I posted something on Facebook or did an interview about my story and they found out, they would attack me regardless of whether Jimmy and I were talking or not.

My relationship with Jimmy was one-sided and it continued to be like that for some time. He has never done anything to me to win my love but I just gave my love to him because I loved him. My Pastor once said that my relationship with Jimmy was not Biblical and that I should end it. I agreed with him because the Bible says in Mathew 19:4–6 that, 'Jesus answered, "Have you not read that from the beginning the Creator 'made them male and female', and said, 'For this reason a man will leave his father and mother and be united to his wife, and the two will become one flesh'? So they are no longer two, but one flesh. Therefore what God has joined together, let man not separate"' Also, Ephesians 5:25–31 says, 'Husbands, love your wives, just as Christ loved the Church and gave Himself up for her to sanctify her, cleansing her by the washing with water through the word, and to present her to Himself as a glorious Church, without stain or wrinkle or any such blemish, but holy and blameless. In the same way, husbands ought to love their wives as their own bodies. He who loves his wife loves himself. Indeed, no one ever hated his own body, but he nourishes and cherishes it, just as Christ does the Church. For we are members of His body.' I didn't end the relationship straight away like the Pastor had suggested because I found it hard to let go of Jimmy and it took me more than two years to finally let go.

I knew right from the beginning that Jimmy was not interested in me romantically and that something was not right in our relationship but I kept making excuses for him and I kept protecting him. Because I thought that if I ignored the bad things in our relationship and only focused on the positive and if only I could work harder, then my relationship with him would be okay but I was deceiving myself. Looking back now, I have realised that I was in love with him and that's why I found it difficult to move on. I have never loved anyone before the same way I loved Jimmy and I feared that I would not be able to love another man again the same way I loved Jimmy. He was my first love. However, in September 2019, I decided that enough was enough and that it was time for me to let go of him and move on with my life, because I knew then that he wasn't coming back home. But I would never stop Jimmy from seeing the girls unless there is a need to.

I gave Jimmy power to do whatever he wanted to do with me because I was trying to be a good wife and I wanted him to feel the love he has never felt or had before, but he threw everything back in my face. I forgot that I needed the same love too and I put his needs first and I forgot about myself. Now that I have let go of him, I finally feel that I have taken back the power. I feel like I am now in control of everything in my life and it feels so good because this time, he and his relatives are not going to hurt or mess me around anymore. I have finally found my voice, strength and confidence and I have started to put myself first. This time, everything is going to be all about me and not him or his relatives.

Eight

RELATIONSHIP CHALLENGES

The best day of 2015 was 2 May because Jimmy was able to declare his love for me in front of our family and friends. Unfortunately, we lost our baby to stillbirth in June that year and things were never the same again in our relationship. I felt and I still feel that Jimmy and his relatives blame me for the loss of our baby and this has played a big role in our relationship breakdown. The day before, a Tuesday morning, we went to the real estate agent to collect the key for our new house that we were going to move into together. We were planning to move in on the weekend but I went into labour that same evening at 6pm and we lost the baby at 6am the following day. Two months after we lost our baby, we moved into our new home together and his relatives all of a sudden stopped coming to my house. They only came if I invited them and they also stopped ringing me to check on how we were doing, apart from Sandy coming to the house to complain about money all the time. Yet they were ringing Jimmy all the time to talk about things that I wasn't allowed to know.

On the surface, everything was perfect in my relationship. It was almost like a fairytale from the outside but on the inside, I was suffocating. I like to talk about things but Jimmy did not want to talk to me and he literally avoided talking to me about anything. He was working late afternoon shifts and came home every night when I was asleep. If he was sleeping in my room that night, he would just sneak into the bed and sleep until morning without saying anything to me and then he would be gone again in the morning. He was never home during the day or at the times that he was not working.

If Jimmy was at home for some reason, he would go to the spare bedroom and stay in bed until it was time to go to work and then he would come out, shower, eat or pack his lunch and go. If he was at home and not sleeping while my daughter and I were watching a movie or a program on TV, he would sit outside to watch sports on the phone or iPad or to chat with other people, particularly women, including his ex-girlfriends. He never sat in the sitting area to watch a movie with us or just to talk like we used to before we moved in together. I wished we hadn't moved in together; I said to myself that if we didn't move in together, maybe we would still be in love. Next time, I will take my time and assess the situation thoroughly before I move in with another man. Sometimes Jimmy would go into the main sitting area and watch a movie or a TV program by himself. And if I went to join him after my daughter had gone to bed at night, he would get up and go to take a shower and then he would go to the kitchen, make a cup of tea for himself and then sit in the family sitting area near the kitchen to drink his tea and watch TV there alone while I waited for him in the main sitting area.

He avoided me in the house at all costs and that made me feel rejected, ugly, unwanted, unloved and worthless. There was only one time when he joined me to watch a movie in the main sitting area after his shower when my daughter had already gone to bed, and I was so happy. He also made a cup of tea for me that night. We were cuddling, kissing and he was rubbing my pregnant tummy. His attention made me feel very special, alive and complete. There were times in our relationship when we cuddled, kissed and shared a bed together but most of the time I slept alone in our room while he slept in one of the other rooms in the house (in the spare bedroom or in the lounge). It was a three-bedroom house with two sitting areas. This is a common practice for many African men where the man sleeps in his own room and the woman sleeps in her own room. He would only come to the woman's room or ask the woman to go into his room if he wanted to be intimate with her. To me this is pure selfishness and I never thought that this kind of a re-lationship where couples sleep in separate rooms would happen to me but it did. However, my own situation was completely different because he wasn't even interested in being intimate with me. If I wanted his touch, I would have to find my own way of getting him in tune. It worked for a short time but I later became exhausted and gave up, and the intimacy never happened again. Every time I tried to initiate intimacy, he would leave me feeling hurt and embarrassed, and I used to think that maybe something was wrong with me which made him find me unattractive and that really hurt.

Jimmy would sometimes go to Sandy's house once or twice a week for some 'family meetings' and he would return at 3am, 4am or even 5am in the morning. What was he doing in his sister's house until that time of the morning? Was he actually in his sister's house or was he somewhere else? One day, he went to my sister's house at 5pm with Sandy after my mother passed away and he came back at 3am in the morning. I asked my sister in the morning what he had been doing there until that time but my sister told me that Jimmy and Sandy were in her house for only thirty minutes and they left her house before 10pm. It was obvious that he went somewhere before they went to my sister's house and after they left her house.

His phone rang and he received messages at all hours of the night. Apart from his ex-girlfriend Jasmine, I didn't know who else was ringing or texting him until I read his messages after he gave his phone to me (as I explain below). I wasn't allowed to touch his phone and his phone had a password that I wasn't allowed to know. For the whole time we were together, I was thinking that Jimmy was having affairs with other women and that he was cheating on me, which is a terrible feeling to have when you are in a relationship. Once I started to have those feelings, my trust for him started to die off gradually. One day, my daughter broke my phone and he gave me one of his phones which confirmed my suspicions. He had two dual sim card phones and I didn't know the reason why he needed two phones. I believe that he used one phone to communicate with one ex-girlfriend and the other phone to communicate with another ex-girlfriend. He bought a new phone and inserted my sim card into the new phone which I thought he was going to give to me but he didn't. He kept my sim card in that new phone in his room for the whole night and then he took the sim card out the following day and inserted it into one of his phones which he then gave to me. He removed the password but he forgot to delete his messages before giving his phone to me.

They were love messages between him, Jasmine and other women in Africa. I believe that God wanted me to know what he was hiding from me and that's why Jimmy ended up giving me his phone without deleting his messages. I read the messages and confronted him about it in September 2015 but he told me that I had nothing to worry or be jealous about because he was married to me and that he was living with me. He said that the fact that he came back home every night indicated that his relationship with those other women was not important, which I found hard to believe, because he wasn't returning home to me every night but to his bedroom. The new phone disappeared a few weeks later and I asked him where it was and he told me that he had given the new phone he bought for me to Jasmine. Apparently, Jasmine's phone fell into the toilet and it stopped working so he gave her our new phone. He even had the guts to bring Jasmine's phone to our house to try and fix it there for her and he thought that was okay.

On another occasion after our third daughter was born and after he had moved out of our family home in June 2016, he went to our local African shop to buy a very beautiful and expensive handbag which he told our friend at the shop that he was buying for me as a present for having a baby, but he never gave the handbag to me. A few weeks later, I went to the same shop and our friend congratulated me for having another baby. He also said that Jimmy was a very good man for buying an expensive handbag as my push present. But he was horrified when I told him that we were separated and that I hadn't received any handbag.

He used to cancel very important meetings or appointments with me just to spend time with his friends or to help his ex-girlfriends. His work was always his first priority, his side of the family was his second priority, his friends were his third priority, and then there was me, his last priority, and that really hurt me a lot. I begged to be wanted, to be hugged, to be cuddled and to be loved but he never loved me back the same way I loved him.

In October 2015, four months after I lost my second daughter to stillbirth, I found out that I was pregnant with my third child, Jimmy's second child. I told him about it and this time around he wasn't overly excited. He told me that he was not ready to have another child with me because he didn't want to see me go through the same pain I went through when we lost our middle baby together. And that he wasn't planning to have any more children with me. His sister Sandy told me a few weeks later that Jimmy had told her that he felt trapped in our relationship because of my pregnancy and that he questioned how I became pregnant again. She said that he wasn't planning to have any more children with me and that they (Jimmy's relatives) would be happier if I didn't have any more children with him, and he eventually moved out in June 2016 after our baby was born. They had tried to make it look like I had cheated on Jimmy by questioning the paternity of my daughter but when my daughter was born, she looked exactly like

Jimmy and some of his relatives. They eventually stopped questioning my daughter's paternity and now they are claiming that she is his daughter and that they want me to hand her over to him. After he moved out, some of his relatives, including his nephews and nieces, had a go at me, saying that I was a bad woman, that I was not the right woman for him and his family, and they also called me all sorts of names. His nephew from interstate rang me to find out what happened between Jimmy and I and he pretended to care about me but after I finished talking with him on the phone, he posted everything I said to him on Facebook without mentioning my name, just to attack and to mock me. I believe that Jimmy's relatives were angry at me because Jimmy left without my children. As mentioned earlier, in South Sudanese culture, children belong to their father and Jimmy's relatives were expecting him to leave with my children but he didn't. They also attacked me after they found out that Jimmy had left without signing our baby's birth certificate, but that was his choice; I didn't put him to it. Jimmy knew all about what his relatives were doing to me but he didn't do anything to stop them from attacking me, instead he told me that I deserved it. If Jimmy had stood by me and if he had treated me well, with respect, his relatives would not have treated me badly the way they did. He instead escalated the situation by telling his relatives everything that was happening between us and he also forwarded angry messages from me to his relatives. They attacked me and held grudges against me because of the angry text messages I sent to him. Jimmy's relatives knew how many text messages I sent to him and the contents of every message. I feel that his relatives misread, misinterpreted and misunderstood my messages. There were four long, angry messages I sent to Jimmy in 2016 after he left but the rest of the messages were good messages about the girls. When Jimmy's relatives started to talk about my messages, every message I have ever sent to Jimmy after he moved out became an evil message, not just angry but evil, and they have never forgiven me for that. They still talk about those messages even more than four years later.

In November 2019 and in January 2020, his niece Abby, Sandy's older daughter, called me names and said that I am 'stupid, confused, delusional, pathetic, childish, public property, psychopathic, manipulative, and a narcissistic kind of a woman with no brain who is always screaming and begging for love'. She said that being highly educated and being a high achiever does not mean that I am smart. She told me to stop clinging onto a relationship that has never worked and will never work because of my attitude. She said that if I had been grateful and had appreciated everything her uncle and his family had done for me, my relationship with her uncle Jimmy would have worked out well but my unappreciative nature has cost me my relationship. Abby wanted me to hand over my daughter, who Jimmy had abandoned, to Jimmy and his relatives so that the chapter between me, him and his relatives could close. They never visited me or helped me with my children or with anything after Jimmy left but now that my daughter is four years old and she is out of nappies, they want me to hand her over to them! Apparently, they are the only people who really love my daughter and know how to take good care of her. Where were they when my daughter was two weeks old after her father left? I asked Abby, but she said that I am 'brain washing' my children and that I am turning my children against them. Abby also told me that if I want Jimmy back to be with me, that I should get rid of my older daughter because 'she does not belong' to them. She said that I should stop forcing my older daughter on Jimmy and his relatives because she is not his daughter.

She made it sound as though Jimmy and his relatives were doing me a favour by him marrying me. The day after my argument with Abby in January 2020, I received a text message from her indicating that Jimmy might have spoken to her and she didn't like what Jimmy told her. She said that I manipulated and coerced her into starting a fight with me to cause division in her family. Jimmy knew about my argument with Abby and I think he might have spoken to her after that. He did apologise to me for Abby's behaviour and he said that I didn't deserve to be called all those names no matter what. I told Abby not to come to my house or anywhere near my children again and I haven't heard from her since. This was the first time that Jimmy had ever stood up for me and I'm sure his relatives didn't like it. If Jimmy had stood up for me from the beginning, I'm sure my relationship with him would not have failed but he has always sided with his relatives and I felt like they were all ganging up on me. I also felt all alone and unloved. Jimmy's relatives have also always sided with him and they treated me like I didn't matter. If they had been neutral, I'm confident that my relationship with Jimmy would still be alive.

In early 2017, Jimmy told me that he had planned to leave me in late 2015 after we had moved in together and after I had started making the decisions in our relationship but he had to stay to help me until our baby was born and that was when he left. I have always treated Jimmy well without judgement. Before Jimmy and I started dating, he had given up on life and that's why when we started dating, he was not working and neither was he studying. It was because of me that Jimmy enrolled himself to study and it was because of me that Jimmy became employed. It was also because of me that Jimmy became a father. If not because of me, I don't know what Jimmy's life would be like now. I gave up a permanent senior mediator job in the country in 2014 for Jimmy and I made a lot of sacrifices for him but he can't even sacrifice a small thing for me! Jimmy enjoyed seeing me in pain and in that kind of emotional torture. He told me that I was a demanding kind of a woman. That I got it all wrong, that he was not avoiding me, and neither was he cheating on me, but that it was all in my head. He told me to suck it up and be like other South Sudanese women here in Adelaide who work two or three jobs, look after their children and husbands and still did all the housework without complaining. I believe that Jimmy was talking about his sister Helen, who fitted the description of all the things he was saying. He might have forgotten that he was talking to a woman with a physical disability who needed support. Regardless of my disability, he should have been there for me as my husband. He said that I had always picked a wrong time to talk to him about things and that if he didn't respond because he was not feeling up to it or because he was tired, that I would make a big deal out of it.

Maybe I did pick a wrong time to talk to him about things but that was the only time he was ever physically present at home. His phone activity also made me become very suspicious of him and he made me become jealous of other women, instead of him making other women become envious and jealous of me. For example, when his phone rang, he would leave the house to go and answer it and talk outside of the house or in his car so I could not hear what he was talking about or who he was talking to. There were times when he went to his car and drove off very fast to a nearby park to return phone calls or simply to make phone calls and he would spend hours at the park talking to people on the phone. To be put into that kind of emotional torture is demoralising, degrading and belittling.

Nine

FINANCIAL HARDSHIP

After Jimmy and I moved in together in 2015, the welfare agency (Centrelink) cancelled my disability support payments three times in a period of four months because Jimmy was working and earning over a certain threshold amount each fortnight, but he didn't tell me. I wasn't reporting his income because I had no income information from him to report to Centrelink. We had two separate bank accounts so I didn't know his income details. I also didn't see his payslips in the house. I only became aware from Centrelink as to how many hours he was working and how much money he was earning fortnightly. In late October that year, Centrelink asked me to report with him to a customer centre office so they could reinstate my payments and we did. This time they had already cancelled my payments twice in three months. Centrelink then found out that they had overpaid me between July and October due to his high income and they asked me to pay back over $3,000. Jimmy knew that I was asked to pay this because of his income but he did not give me any money to help me pay it back. Instead he became very angry that I had found out from Centrelink that he had not been honest with me about his job and his income, so he moved out of our bedroom into the spare bedroom to sleep there permanently. And that was just the beginning of the end of my marriage. Even though we did not move in together until two months later, Centrelink used the date we signed our lease agreement to calculate how much money I was entitled to.

On the outside we were a very happy married couple, but on the inside we were not a married couple anymore as we were already living two separate lives under the same roof but we didn't want people to know. We lived in the same house but in separate bedrooms until early 2016. During this time, Jimmy distanced himself from me completely and he refused to tell me his income so I could report it to Centrelink. Centrelink had instructed me to report his income to them to determine my ongoing disability support payments but he ignored this, so Centrelink cancelled my payments again.

This time, he refused to go to Centrelink with me to sort out my payments. Instead he told me that it was my problem and that I should deal with it on my own. He was not happy because he was the one paying the rent and yet Centrelink was paying the rental assistance money

($150) into my account fortnightly. I asked Centrelink to pay the rental assistance money to him but they couldn't because the rental assistance is usually paid as part of the Family Tax Benefit, which can only be paid to the child's primary caregiver, which was me. I offered to give the rental assistance money to him to resolve the problem but he said no. Because I didn't have enough money for food, bills and for my daughter's childcare fees, and also because we were no longer living together as husband and wife, I decided to go to Centrelink to ask for a separation form, which I brought to him. Jimmy was happy to complete and sign the separation form and he even returned it to Centrelink himself which resulted in my payments being reinstated in full. But now he is saying that the reason why he moved out of home seven months later and did not return was because he felt embarrassed and humiliated after signing the separation form. He says that he has lost respect and support from people in our community because of signing that Centrelink form and because of moving out of our family home. He also says that people, especially men, in our community are saying a lot of bad things about him, stating that he is a bad and a mean man for not treating me well and for not providing for me and my children. He feels embarrassed going into the community now because people are saying that he is not man enough because he listened to and took his sisters' advice when they told him to move out. The men in our community said that Jimmy should have listened to me, his wife, and made the right decision, which was to stay with me and my children. Even if it meant that his relatives would not talk to him for some time because of his decision, they would come around with time, they said.

Signing the separation form was not easy for me but the decision had to be made to stop me from stressing over money and potentially losing my third baby. There are a lot of women in Australia, especially South Sudanese women with limited English skills, who are going through similar financial difficulties and stress caused by their husband's or partner's selfishness, but often these issues are not spoken of. Many women are suffering in silence and are repaying huge amounts of money back to Centrelink because of overpayments that could have been easily avoided if their partners were honest and transparent with their income.

Very soon every conversation with Sandy became about money, money and money. Starting from a few days after we signed the separation form in 2015, Sandy came to my house a few times to complain about money. She told me that it was not fair that I allowed her brother, Jimmy, to pay the rent by himself yet he didn't have money. She said that Jimmy and I should go halves in the rent given that the lease agreement was in both our names, in order to resolve the money problem we were having.

Jimmy and I had agreed before we started looking for the house that he would pay the rent and I would pay for food, bills (electricity, telephone, internet and water) and my daughter's childcare fees until his work hours were increased and then he would pay rent and part of the bills, which he later did after our Centrelink visit. I was receiving $800 of disability support payments plus $400 of family payments, including rental assistance, from Centrelink a fortnight after I stopped working but I was spending more on food, bills and child care compared to the money he was spending on rent, yet his sister Sandy still wanted me to pay half of the rent on top of everything else. Whenever I requested that the three of us (Sandy, Jimmy and me) should sit and talk about the things she was complaining about and to also talk about the things that were making our relationship fall apart, Sandy would organise a general family meeting in her house or in her sister Helen's house where she would invite Jimmy and her other relatives and then they would talk without my knowledge. I would then hear about the meeting days or weeks later. I wasn't invited to the meeting that had something to do with my relationship with Jimmy and I was not informed of what was discussed and the outcome of the discussion.

I was working as a project coordinator for most of 2015 but in December I had a fall and broke my ankle and I couldn't go back to work in 2016. I tried to work from home for a short period of time but because part of my role involved facilitating group activities, information sessions and the stakeholders' quarterly face-to-face meetings, I couldn't work from home long term. So my CEO and I agreed that I should take time off work without pay and focus on my pregnancy and also my recovery. Because I was heavily pregnant after the Christmas and New Year's break, I couldn't return to work so I stayed home and relied solely on Centrelink payments. I had been working two days a week and receiving $800 a fortnight in salary plus $200 of disability support payments as well as family payments each fortnight.

In January 2016, I started to look for another house to move into and raise my children because my relationship with Jimmy and his relatives had become very toxic due to the money issue. Money is a number one relationship killer in Australia, especially amoung South Sudanese families. Another reason for wanting to move was that, one day, my wheelchair became stuck in the gravel on the driveway after returning home from the shop and there was nobody to help me. It took me an hour to increase the wheelchair's speed to maximum and then wheel away really fast to be able to get out of the gravel. We had asked the landlord weeks earlier to put concrete on the driveway but they didn't. The plan was for me to find another house with a good driveway and put the lease under my name and then it would be up to Jimmy to decide whether to move in with us and pay half of the rent or if he would go and look for his own accommodation and help me from there, to put an end to sister Sandy's constant financial complaints. I discussed it with Jimmy first and he agreed that he would move in with us once the contract in the other house was finished, so he could help me with the rent and bills. I just want to point out that all these things, including the separation, were happening when I was still deeply in love with Jimmy. I find that when you love someone, it doesn't matter what that person does to you, you will always love them. Your feelings towards them may change to a degree but you will always love them. You may not see eye to eye sometimes, talk to each other or even live together, but the love will always be there.

One thing I have learnt from my relationship with Jimmy is that African men are always the ones controlling love, not the women. I also now know that for a relationship to work, the man should be the one always to love the woman more than the woman loves him and be chasing after her, but if the woman is the one that loves the man more and chases after him, like I did, it doesn't matter what the woman does, the man will not budge. I was speaking to a friend in 2017 and he said that women always make a big mistake by becoming pregnant to men who don't love them, thinking that when they become pregnant with his child that he will all of a sudden love them but it doesn't work that way. He said that, 'if the man doesn't love you, fall pregnant for him and you will see how badly he will treat you'. He went as far as saying that 'men do not love women because they have children together but they love women who they know are wife material — are weak and willing to submit to them or are willing to obey them and be controlled by them'. He concluded by saying that 'if a man feels threatened by the woman's personality, successes, achievements, education, income or job roles, that man will not stop loving the woman but he will run as far away as he can from that woman'. And I think that he was in part right, drawing from my own personal relationship experience with Jimmy. I believe that, apart from the disability stigma, the loss of our middle child, our financial hardship, and his relatives' interference in our relationship, my education and achievements were part of the reasons why my relationship with Jimmy failed. The red flags were there from the beginning but I ignored them. I thought that if I worked harder in our relationship, things would go back to normal, whatever that looks like. I thought that I wasn't doing enough in our relationship and that's why my relationship was falling apart but I later realised that all that was happening had nothing to do with what I did or didn't do but it was all about him and his insecurities. I also learnt that relationships are two-way traffic where both parties have to work equally as hard to make the relationship work.

Nothing I could have done was going to fix my relationship. I believe that counselling, therapy and prayers would have saved my marriage but Jimmy left way too early before these were implemented. He didn't even try to fix the problem or compromise with me, but he just left. After we lost our baby, he and I attended a few grief and loss counselling therapy sessions through a psychologist to help us deal with the loss of our daughter, as suggested by the doctors at the Women's and Children's Hospital in Adelaide. The therapy worked for a short time but then Jimmy decided to stop going. From that time on, the gap between him and me started to grow bigger and bigger and I didn't know why. A lot of people, especially men and people from my own South Sudanese community, avoid talking about issues to professionals, particularly when it comes to family relationships, and they tend to sweep them under the carpet not knowing that one day those issues will become a very big problem that will be hard for them to resolve. South Sudanese people instead feel more comfortable involving the community in private family matters to try to resolve the issue rather than seeking professional help confidentially. In most cases, some individuals in the community will escalate the problem and will instead break those relationships further by making up stories and spreading rumours.

There were also things in our relationship that we both needed to talk to a professional about who would not judge us and that's why Jimmy and I saw a counsellor together. But after Sandy found out that he was attending counselling with me, she rang me and spoke to me in a very angry voice. She said that there was nothing wrong with Jimmy mentally or emotionally that necessitated me having to drag him into seeing a psychologist. She said that if I was mentally ill and I needed to see a psychologist to attend brain therapy, I should go alone but I should leave her brother out of it. She also said that nobody in her family had ever been diagnosed with mental health issues and that no outsider had ever accused any of her family members of being mentally ill. She has always referred to me as an outsider when Jimmy and I were not talking, and because I was an outsider to her, there were things in their family that I wasn't allowed to know or be part of. But when Jimmy and I were talking, she would refer to me as 'Mulamu', which means in-law in Luganda (a language in Uganda).

For example, when her children were graduating from high school and university, I was not invited. Jimmy was invited and he went alone without me. One day, she found out that Jimmy had revealed some information to me about himself that she wasn't aware of and without telling her first. Anything that Jimmy told me has always been second-hand information. He had to discuss anything about him or us with Sandy first before he could discuss it with me. Sandy had to know everything about us, including our bedroom business. After she found out what Jimmy had told me, she asked how come I, the outsider, knew about that information first and they, the family, had not been informed? It was kind of like a case of a trophy wife where my role as trophy wife was only to bring trophies into the family and then leave. And when I stopped bringing trophies into the family, then I was no longer needed. I stopped taking Jimmy to therapy with me and I also stopped encouraging him to seek professional help after Sandy's confrontation.

In late March 2016, we found a three-bedroom house and we put the lease under my name as agreed and then my daughter and I moved in. Jimmy and our friends helped us with moving into our new house but he remained in our old house until late May after the contract was finished there. He visited us on a regular basis and he also helped me with transporting my daughter to school. In late May, when I was in the hospital with my third newborn daughter, Jimmy moved into our new house but he was only there for two weeks and then he moved out indefinitely.

In April 2016, after Jimmy's relatives found out that I had moved into a house that was under my name, Sandy came to my house to complain again. This time she came to blame me for breaking up my marriage and splitting up my family and she condemned me for not including Jimmy's name on the new lease. This time I wasn't going to sit there and listen to her complaints so I asked her to leave and she did. I was heavily pregnant, exhausted and I had no energy for any drama. It's not good to live in a crowded relationship where so many people are always competing for the attention of the man at the centre because, no matter what you do, nothing will ever change unless the partner who is bringing the crowd into the relationship decides to get rid of that crowd.

Ten

THE DAY MY FAMILY
FELL APART

Two weeks after our third daughter was born, my world turned upside down when my family completely fell apart. That morning, Jimmy woke up and completed his morning routine as usual; brushing his teeth, helping me in the kitchen with the dishes, cleaning the garden in the front of the house, having a shower, getting dressed, having morning tea and then going to work. We had concrete paving at the back of the house and on the sides of the house with a concrete driveway leading into the carport and a concrete walk way from the driveway leading into the front entrance. There was only a small garden in front of the house which he pulled the weeds out of. He then told me that he was going to pay our bills at the local post office and he would go to work thereafter. He gave the children and me a kiss and off he went. But there was something different about him this particular morning. Usually he would shower our five-year-old daughter, help her dress and he would bring me a cup of tea or a bowl of porridge in our room at 6am for me to have after breastfeeding the baby, but he didn't do that on that day. I had been having a big cup of tea or porridge in bed every morning, before I left the room, since we came back from the hospital with our newborn baby because my body was weak and shaky. This was due to the loss of too much blood during my caesarean section. I had to drink a lot of water and then go to the kitchen to get the porridge myself that morning. I asked him to help shower our five-year-old daughter but he told me in a very angry and rude voice to shower her myself and that if I could not shower her, then she should go and shower herself. I thought that he was joking but he actually meant it. So I showered her myself. It was still too early for me to bend and pick up things from the floor due to the painful caesarean wound but I had no choice than to bend and shower my daughter in the bath.

Even though he was clearly agitated that morning and things didn't seem normal, I didn't pay close attention to him and his mood as our baby was crying and I had to attend to her. Little did I know that Jimmy had not only checked out of our relationship four days earlier (eleven days after our daughter was born) when he moved out of our bedroom but he had also checked out of our family home that morning! I later found out that he had packed some things out of our house into his car early that morning while I was still sleeping. It was clear that he had been planning to leave for a long time. But I believe he was torn between leaving and staying as he had not been sleeping for the two nights before he left. He watched TV until morning two nights before he left. His decision to leave was starting to haunt him that morning and that was why he was getting more and more agitated as the morning progressed.

When I came back from the hospital and found that Jimmy had moved in with us, I was so happy and I thought that he had come back home to live with us for good. I also thought that things were going to go back to normal in our relationship, but things were soon going to take a turn for the worse. He had even moved back into my room for a week to help bring our baby to me in the night and put her back to her bed after I had finished breastfeeding her and changing her nappy. She slept in my room in her own bed beside my bed. When Jimmy moved out of our room again, I didn't think that he was planning to leave and I didn't think much of it because we had always slept in different rooms. He was in the spare bedroom for four days and then he moved out. I was so blinded by the love I had for him and by the fact that he was so affectionate to me after our daughter was born and after he moved in with us. He had never been like that before. What I didn't know was that the kiss he gave me and our daughters that morning was a goodbye kiss. If I had known that he was not coming back home that night, I would have tried to talk to him that morning before he went to work to try and resolve the problem but I didn't know. It was a beautiful Saturday morning at 11:30am when he left home for work. Usually he would pack lunch as he was working late afternoon shifts but on this particular day he did not take any food with him. Also, he would usually ring at 6:30pm before our five-year-old daughter went to bed to tell her that he loved her and to wish her a good night, but he didn't ring. My daughter waited and waited for his call in vain, and he didn't call. I rang him a few times but he didn't answer. This is unlike him, I said to myself. She cried and cried but I told her that it was okay. I said that daddy was probably very busy at work and we prayed together and then she went to bed expecting to see daddy in the morning so they could go to Church together.

I went to bed that night and woke up at 11pm to the sound of my baby crying. Then I saw a text message from him stating that he wasn't coming home. I panicked and I rang him after I had finished breastfeeding my baby and changing her nappy to check if he was okay and what he meant by he wasn't coming back home. We talked for about ten minutes on the phone and he told me that there was nothing wrong but that he wasn't coming back home that night because he was going to a nightclub with some friends. I asked him if someone was having a birthday party at the pub and he said no. I thought it was rather odd to go to a nightclub for someone who doesn't drink alcohol and for someone who has never been to a nightclub before but he told me that it was time for him to start doing new things in his life.

When I first started dating Jimmy, I thought that he was a devoted Christian but I soon found out that he was anti churches; not anti-Christ but anti churches. The first time I went to his house, I saw Bible verses pinned on his kitchen wall and on the fridge. Also the first time he slept in my house, he asked me to pray first before we went to bed and that was what made me think that he was a devoted Christian. But the way he talked made me think that he was not a Christian. I later found out that he had not been to Church for a very long period of time before we started dating. I encouraged him to go back to Church and he finally started going to Church with us soon after we moved in together. He continued going to Church even after he had moved out of our family home for some time and then he stopped going to Church all together. I pleaded with him to come back home that night so we could talk about whatever it was that was making him not want to come back home, but he reassured me that there was nothing wrong to talk about and he told me to go back to sleep. He sounded happy on the phone, but how could I go to sleep not knowing where he was, who he was with and what he was doing? I wish I had known the reason why he chose to go to a nightclub and why he was not coming back home that night, so I could try and resolve the problem sooner.

I prayed, rebuking the devil, saying that the devil is a liar and that my husband will be back home, and then I went back to bed. I was awake for most of that night, with a crying baby in my arms and with a very painful caesarean wound. My ankle was also not properly healed when Jimmy left (Chapter 1 and 9 has more information about my ankle). He came back home the following day, looking like he had been run over by a truck. He sat at the dining table and dozed off to sleep for about five minutes. He was a mess when he woke up! He looked like he had lost something or rather he was lost. I saw the guilt in his eyes but before I could say a word to him, he was off to our bedroom to collect a few of his clothes and shoes and he went to the carport to collect a few more things and then he left the house. He packed the things into his car, which was parked out on the street in front of the house. He then came back to the house to take more things and I asked him what was going on but he said nothing. I asked him again for the second time and he looked me in the eye, smiled, he told me that there was nothing wrong, and then he walked away. I saw the lies in his eyes but he was so determined not to tell me what was really going on.

Before he left the house with his things that afternoon, he told me that he would be back in the evening and that we would talk then. And yes, he did come back that evening for a few minutes and he left again without telling me anything. He appeared restless when he returned in the evening and he rushed out of the house so quickly as though something was chasing him but he came back a few minutes later and we had dinner together with his nephew Ryan and Ryan's girlfriend, who came to visit us.

I went to bed at 7:30pm shortly after my children had gone to sleep and I left Jimmy and his nephew to watch a movie. At about 9:30pm, he came to my bedroom and told me that he was going back to where he slept the night before.

'Where did you sleep last night?' I asked.

'In Ryan's house,' he replied.

'Why did you go to sleep in Ryan's house when you have a home here?' I asked but he was quiet. 'I thought Ryan and his girlfriend live in a one-bedroom unit,' I added.

'Yes,' he said.

'So where did you sleep?' I asked.

'In his house,' he said.

'Where was Ryan?' I asked.

'He moved in with his girlfriend and nobody lives in his house at the moment,' he said.

'So this sleepover thing in Ryan's house, is that a

temporary thing or a permanent sleeping arrangement?' I asked.

'Go to sleep and we will talk in the morning,' he said and he walked out of the room and then out of the house!

Why did Jimmy come back to my house that evening if he was not ready to talk to me? Could it be that he was guilty of something? Did he care about me and our children? Or did he simply come back to see if I had crumbled so that he could laugh at me? I asked myself all these questions and I went back to sleep. It was a Sunday night.

Jimmy came back on Monday morning to drop our five-year-old daughter to school and he took me and our baby to the GP later that morning for our baby's two-week follow-up appointment. When we came back to the house after the GP visit, he washed our dishes, packed his lunch and off he went to work. This time, although he was chatty and cheerful, he kept his distance from me and I still didn't know where he spent the last two nights and where his clothes and other things were. I was starting to regain confidence in myself after I saw a positive change in him that afternoon, thinking that he was going to come back home after work that night, but he didn't. I went to bed that Monday night at 7:30pm happy and expecting to see him in the house after work but I woke up at 11:30pm again with my baby crying and he was not in the spare bedroom. I came out of the bedroom after feeding my daughter and changing her nappy and looked for him everywhere, calling out, 'Babe, where are you?' But there was no response and there was no sign of him anywhere in the house. My hands were sweaty and I started to panic again and my weak body began to tremble. I looked in our daughter's bedroom and saw that she was sound asleep. I went back to my room, took a deep breath and I rang him. We talked for about thirty minutes on the phone but he still didn't tell me where he was, what he was doing, who he was with and why he left. He sounded very happy on the phone and he was even laughing while talking to me. That laughter on the phone made me very angry.

I had no reason to laugh with him or at him but I had a lot of reasons to cry on the phone. He later told me that he was laughing at me on the phone because he had finally got me where he wanted me to be and that he enjoyed hearing my panicky voice. He thought I wouldn't miss him when he was gone but knowing that I loved him and I missed him a lot made him feel better, he said. I told him to come back home so we could talk face to face but he told me that he wasn't coming back to be with me ever again and he refused to tell me the reason why. He also said that he owed me nothing and that I owed him nothing and that because of that, he didn't feel obliged to give me an explanation about his whereabouts and why he was not coming back home.

He didn't console me when I was crying on the phone like he used to but he kept laughing. It was like he was rejoicing in my agony and it felt like an 'I got you' moment. I wish I had known what I had done wrong so I could fix it and have him back home with me and my children but that was not going to happen. He came back the following day to drop our daughter to school and he pretended like everything was okay. He walked past my bedroom and went straight to the kitchen to watch my daughter eat her breakfast. He greeted me, saying 'good morning' while walking past. I was changing our baby's nappy but he didn't stop at the door to check on our baby or ask how she was doing. A few minutes later, I heard him shouting in the kitchen at my daughter to hurry up, which was unusual. He had never yelled or shouted at my daughter before and that really scared me. He always came to get my daughter when she was dressed in her uniform and eating her breakfast.

My daughter had to learn to shower herself every morning with limited supervision from me sometimes. If I was feeding the baby, changing the baby's nappy or even getting her breakfast ready, she would have to shower herself with instructions from me but without supervision. That Tuesday evening, he picked our daughter up from school and he helped me with serving her dinner. I was cooking porridge and I asked him to stay so we could talk and he stayed for an hour but he didn't eat.

I asked him what was happening but he said that there was nothing wrong. I then asked him to come back home and he told me that he wasn't coming back home to live with me again. I asked why and he told me to answer that question myself. He said that I already knew the answer to the question I was asking him.

I asked what was going to happen with our baby, our rent and our bills and he told me that he couldn't take her because he was not able to look after her single-handedly. He also said that he was looking to settle down with another woman and that when that happened, he would come and take our baby to live with him and that his new woman would look after our baby. I told him that I would never refuse him to have access to our children but he would never take our baby to live with him and to be looked after by another woman full time. I wasn't asking for him to take our baby but he responded that he would take her once he was settled with another woman. He also said that he was not able to have our children in his house for a weekend or even a few hours a week because the place where he was living was not suitable for children. It was clear that he didn't want to have anything to do with my children and he just had to get himself out of my house as soon as possible by avoiding talking to me about our children. Before he left the house that evening, he told me to manage my rent and bills by myself. He was calm that evening but he looked worried. A few weeks later, I found out that he had lost all his permanent shifts a couple of days after he moved out of our family home and that he was back on a few casual shifts here and there just like when he first started working.

He came the following day, Wednesday, to drop our daughter to school but he came very late and this time he didn't say good morning to me and he didn't even ask how our baby was. He sometimes came to the house three or four times a day after he had moved out just for three to five minutes and then he would be gone without saying or taking anything. Even when the baby was in the bassinet in the lounge area, he would walk past the bassinet so many times without looking in to check on the baby. He never cuddled our baby and he was becoming more and more distant from her. He had even become forgetful and he was leaving his phones in my house in the mornings when he came to drop our daughter to school but he picked them up afterwards. He had never left his phones anywhere in the house before when we were living together but now that we are no longer living together he was leaving his phones in my house for hours. One of his phones even had the password removed. I couldn't help but snoop through his phone and read his messages. I knew that it was a wrong thing to do snooping around his phones but I just had to find out what was going on. His phone had also been ringing for more than five times and that was when I got tempted to see who was ringing.

I read the messages and left the phones back on the bench where he had left them. He came back and took his phones in a hurry.

That Wednesday morning he appeared stressed and confused but I allowed him to take my daughter to school anyway while I was still making alternative arrangements for her school drop-off. I was becoming increasingly worried about the state of his mental health as he wasn't talking to me about what he was thinking and I didn't know what he was planning to do next. I had to work out something fast to stop him from dropping my daughter to school and from letting himself back into our house whenever he felt like it. Just before 6am the next morning, I heard the shower running and I went to check but the bathroom door was locked and the lights were on in the bathroom. I knew then that it was him in my shower and, sure enough, a few minutes later he came out of my bathroom with his work backpack. He still had the keys to my house. I need to take those keys off him fast, I said to myself. I thought it was disrespectful of him to come to my house and shower in my bathroom and even use my towels after he had moved out of my house days earlier and after telling me that he was never coming back to live with me again.

He took my daughter to school that morning, came back and parked my car in front of the house and then he left. He had always used my car to transport my daughter to and from school if I was not using the car and he had the spare car key. Usually after dropping my daughter off, he would come back to the house and collect a few things or just walk from one room to the next before going back to where he was living but that Thursday morning, he didn't come back to the house. On Friday he came in the morning and I took my keys off him. He was very angry after he handed the keys over and he left my house in a hurry. He later accused me of locking him 'out of our house'. In the South Sudanese Kuku culture, if a woman is accused of locking her man out, the elders of the community would gather together to talk about it, the woman would be fined and then some traditional rituals would be performed before that man could be allowed back into the house. I didn't know what was in his mind when he accused me of locking him out of our family home.

Eleven

THE DAY HE MOVED OUT

The next time I saw Jimmy was a week later when he came to collect more things, including things that most South Sudanese men would not take if they were moving out of their family homes, especially if children are involved. He took a bed, blankets, bedsheets, TV, our outdoor chairs, kitchen stuff including our cooking pots, cups, plates and other small things, leaving our children and me with barely anything but huge bills and expensive rent to pay. I had to start from zero again but I bounced back so quickly and I replaced the things he took and also bought more new things for my house. I had sent him a text message a few days earlier asking him to come and collect his books and a few of his personal belongings from the spare bedroom because I wanted to use the room to store the baby's things. I didn't know that he was going to come and take everything and leave us with nothing. Instead he left the books that I had asked him to come and collect. He had five boxes of storybooks, educational books and novels in my spare bedroom. He used to love reading.

When he was moving the things out of the house into a big truck that was parked out on the side of the road, I tried to talk to him in the bedroom while he was taking the bed apart and I tried to stop him from packing our things up without discussing with me but he became very angry, intimidating, very aggressive and he cornered me in the room. He said a few words and, honestly, I don't remember the exact words that were said. He scared the daylights out of me that day and that was the second time he had done that. Ryan was also there helping him to move the things out of our house and I told him to stop but Jimmy became even more aggressive and he yelled at me. I left the room immediately and watched him walk through that door with our things but I could do nothing to stop him. I could have handled things differently to stop him from taking our things that day but I didn't. I could have called the police when he was being aggressive towards me on a number of occasions but I didn't. From that moment, I realised that I had lost my best friend, my husband and the father of my children. The reality of the matter had started to sink in. The man that I loved and the man I married was gone in the blink of an eye, just like that, leaving me with a two-week-old baby girl, a five-year-old daughter and a very painful caesarean wound to nurture. What did I ever do wrong to deserve this? How did we get here? And why didn't I see this coming? What am I going to tell the kids? How am I going to explain this to them? I asked myself all these questions while crying.

Jimmy had been really rude and aggressive towards me earlier in the week before he left for work that Saturday morning and didn't return but he apologised two days later for speaking to me in that manner. He had cornered me and verbally attacked me on the couch near our sleeping baby, who was seven days old at the time. He blamed me for choosing our newborn's name. He said that everyone in his family had named their firstborn daughters after his grandmother and that he was the only one who had not named his first daughter after his grandmother. Culturally, South Sudanese people name their children after their grandparents. He felt that I had robbed him of that right as the man of the house to name his child, which I understood but, wait a minute, was he forgetting something that soon? A month before our daughter was born, I asked him on a number of occasions to choose a name for our baby but he didn't say anything. I told him that before the doctors could operate on me, they would ask for the baby's name first, and that was what they did with my first child. I insisted that we choose the name and agree on it before we went to the hospital but he didn't give me any name. After we had lost our middle daughter at the hospital, he refused to name her; instead, he told me to name her but I didn't. We stayed at the hospital from 6am to 4pm waiting for him to name our daughter before we could leave her with the midwife but he didn't. At a few minutes to 4pm, I gave the name Hannah to the midwife and Sandy gave the midwife Jimmy's last name and then we left. He later told me in 2017 that he thought it was rather strange that I would talk to him about baby names. He said that, traditionally, people don't talk about baby names before the baby is born and that it is not women's position to talk about baby names. He said that my role as a woman was to go to the hospital, have the baby, come back home and then the father of the baby would choose the baby's name a week after the birth.

I told him that things are done differently here compared to back home in South Sudan and he should have said something before the baby was born so I could know but he didn't. I also reminded him that when we had just arrived in the operation room, he disappeared for more than an hour and he returned when the doctors were just about to take the baby out of my tummy. We couldn't wait for him any longer as I was having an emergency caesarean so I gave the doctors the name. He said that he had to go and put our bags in the locker but when he returned, he couldn't find anybody to take him to the theatre sooner, which I find hard to believe because there were midwives at the reception desk near the public locker and there were also hospital volunteers everywhere to take people wherever they wanted to go within the hospital. We all went to the theatre together and he saw the operation room where I was before he left. He told me that he was going to make a phone call in the next room but he didn't return until more than an hour later. He also had my phone so I couldn't ring him. I also reminded him that after we had been discharged from the hospital, I had told him that he could change the baby's name to the name he wanted to go on the birth certificate but he refused to change the name and he refused to sign our baby's birth certificate. He instead said that if his sister Sandy told him to change the name and to sign the birth certificate, then he would do it, but if his sister said no, he would not do it. It took me two months of running around to find the right information to enable me to register our daughter with the births registration office in Adelaide without his signature after he had refused to sign our daughter's birth certificate. Some people may disagree with me but I thought that it was rather selfish of him to ask me to name our dead baby and for him to want to name our living baby.

I asked him, what does Sandy have to do with our daughter's birth certificate? He said that I was being disrespectful of the only mother figure woman he had known since his mother died. He also said that he owed his life to his sister Sandy for bringing him up and for everything she had done in his life including bringing him to Australia. He concluded by saying that he would always do whatever his sister told him to do whether I liked it or not. I said to him that I was not against his relationship with his sister but what I didn't understand was why she should make decisions about our relationship and about our baby's birth certificate but he said nothing. I knew that he had tried to run away from the hospital before our baby was born and that's why he disappeared for more than an hour. Months earlier he had asked me who was going to the hospital with me when I would be having our baby and who was going to look after our five-year-old daughter at home while I was at the hospital! He said that he would not go to the hospital with me and that he would not take time off work to look after our five-year-old daughter. After saying those things to me, I arranged for a friend to come with me to the hospital and another friend to look after my daughter but because I went into labour three weeks early and at 2am, Jimmy had to come to the hospital with me and Sandy had to look after my five-year-old daughter for five hours that day. I tried ringing my friends in the night so many times but they didn't answer and they didn't ring me back until later that afternoon.

When he cornered and verbally attacked me at home near our sleeping baby, I didn't take it very seriously as I thought that maybe the stress of having a newborn baby in the house had gotten to him, but he meant business. I later discovered that Jimmy had already packed a few things out of our house, including our five-year-old daughter's things, like her favourite DVDs, toys and some of her personal things, when I was still in the hospital with our newborn baby. He had planned to leave with my children but something changed after we came back home from the hospital and he decided to leave alone. Perhaps the crying new baby changed his mind, I said to myself. Why did Jimmy run away after the birth of his child? Why did he abandon the baby that was born alive after the tragic death of his first child? I asked myself these questions but I will never really get the answers until he tells me.

We did have a few misunderstandings, disagreements and arguments in the past before I became pregnant with our third child and before she was born, as all couples do, but nothing too serious and those misunderstandings, disagreements and arguments were not strong enough reasons for him to leave. They were instead strong reasons for me to leave but I didn't.

When Jimmy finally started to talk about the reasons why he left, everything became my fault. It was my fault that he left, my fault that he didn't return, and it was my fault that he was aggressive towards me before he moved out. I had even started to believe that it was my fault that he left and my fault that he was rude and aggressive towards me on a number of occasions. In that moment, I started to second guess myself and I started to lose confidence in myself again. Fear had become my companion and I felt guilty and embarrassed for the failure of my marriage. The strong, vibrant and outspoken woman that I was had become shy, quiet, withdrawn and lacking confidence. I had lost myself because of love and I didn't know who I was anymore. But I bounced back strong, confident and more outspoken than I had ever been. In all honesty, I didn't deserve the kind of treatment Jimmy and his relatives gave me, no matter what. And no woman should have to go through what I went through. I entered into a relationship with Jimmy to find love and to hopefully live happily ever after but I didn't find the love I was looking for. I did, however, find myself and I got children out of that relationship even though one baby is growing up in heaven. I picked myself up, put the scattered pieces of my life back together, wrote and published my first book, *Beyond Calamity*, in the midst of all the hurt, pain and agony, and the bittersweet thing was that Jimmy and his relatives came to celebrate my success with me during my book launch in June 2019.

Sandy slept in my house the night before my book launch. She came to my house that day to help me with cooking food for the launch and she also came to plead with me to give Jimmy another chance. She said that even if we didn't get to have any more children, they would be okay with that as long as Jimmy and I reconciled and became a family again. I was happy that Jimmy and his relatives supported me during my book launch; that was the first time I have ever felt loved and appreciated by Jimmy and his relatives. I was also sad that I had to do something like publishing a book for Jimmy and his relatives to love and appreciate me on the day of my book launch. Why can't he just love me the way I am? I asked myself. If Jimmy had told me on the day of the launch that he loved me and that he was proud of me, we would have been back together since then but he didn't. After my book launch, I asked him to come back to my place that night and help me carry some things but he told me that he had work to do very early the following morning and he left.

I have been waiting for Jimmy to tell me that he loves me and our children and that he wants to come back home but I feel like he thinks that he is too special to say those words. All he has been telling me since June 2016 is that he isn't coming back home to live with me again and that I should find for myself another man and move on with my life. I don't want to hear Sandy or anyone else tell me to give Jimmy another chance and take him back; I want to hear Jimmy tell me those things himself. If Jimmy had told me before September 2019 that he wanted to come back home, I would have taken him back.

I told him that if he did not believe that I needed an apology because I have a disability and because I mean nothing to him, he should at least say sorry to our children for abandoning them but he said that he had done nothing wrong to our children. According to him, I am the person to apologise to our children for making him leave and for making him not return home. Jimmy has made me and my children feel too dirty to live with him or even come close to him. Sometimes I think that he feels too special to have me and my children in his life.

Twelve

EMOTIONAL STRUGGLE AFTER MY RELATIONSHIP BREAKDOWN

Jimmy is gone and now begins the emotional journey of my life. I was emotionally strong for a few weeks to begin with but things started to go downhill from there for a period of time. Why am I not angry? I should be smashing things in the house but I am not! Did I really want Jimmy to leave? Am I happy that he is gone? All these questions were running through my head but the answer is no, I wasn't happy. I was still dealing with the emotions of having a newborn baby and the death of my mother two days before my third daughter was born. My hormones were all over the place, as any new mum would know, and my reaction to the whole situation was numbness. Maybe this was the reason why I was strong to start with, I said to myself.

I was breastfeeding. This time I had more breast milk compared to when I had my first child. My clothes were always getting wet and in the night my bed was wet too with dripping milk from my nipples. One thing I was worried about was losing my breast milk and not being able to look after my children if I ever got into a state of stress, anxiety or even depression. As weeks passed, I started to stay awake in the bed most nights. I know what you are thinking. You are probably thinking that my baby was not sleeping, but that was not the reason. My baby cried for a few weeks and she quickly settled and got into routine. She is a good eater and a good sleeper. She sleeps through the night and she wasn't crying when I was having the sleepless nights.

I laid in the bed staring at the ceiling most nights, thinking of the good times Jimmy and I shared together. My mind had become a music library playlist and it played the good memories over and over again. I also re-membered the emotional torture he put me through and I wondered what I had ever done to deserve that. I couldn't get Jimmy off my mind! What was wrong with me? Was I losing my mind? I asked myself. No. I wanted Jimmy back. I loved him. He was my rock and a shoulder for me to lean and to cry on during the darkest times of my life and he was my comforter when we lost our second daughter to stillbirth. I felt empty and I became fearful of so many things after we lost our baby but Jimmy was there for me. He always knew how to say the right words at the right time. I was not sure if I could get through without him this time. I thought that I was alone, but God was right there with me and by my side the whole time, and God brought me through the valley and out to the other side.

Jimmy would answer my calls sometimes and he always sounded very happy on the phone but he didn't say the right things to me anymore. I wanted him to tell me that he missed me, that he missed our children and that he still loved me but he didn't say it. I was left guessing what might be going through his head. Does he still love me? I asked myself. Not knowing what he was thinking, what he was doing and what he was planning to do next drove me crazy. The only way to cope with the situation at the time was for me to send him angry words in text messages, saying that because he left me at a time when I needed him most, that he would never find another woman like me, that he would never be happy without me, and that he would suffer for the rest of his life. I also told him that I was happy because our children were with me and not with him and that, if I wanted, I could stop him from seeing the girls, but saying those things didn't make me feel any better. I wanted him to respond but he instead ignored my text messages and he also started to ignore my calls from November 2016 for a period of four months. The only text message I received from him in late 2016 stated that, 'if you don't have anything to do with your time, go to sleep and please stop sending me such messages because I am tired of laughing at your messages'. There I was pouring my heart out to him but he was laughing! What kind of a person does that? I asked. The messages I sent to him were not all angry; there were also good messages with pictures of our children to update him on how our girls were doing.

Nevertheless, I refused to give up and I continued ringing him. This time he answered and he told me to leave him alone and to stay away from him and his new woman! He said that he did not want to have anything to do with me and my children because I didn't need him in my life anymore. What did he mean by I didn't need him anymore? I asked. How many times have I asked him to come back home and he said that he was never coming back to be with me. Why was I ringing and texting him if I didn't want him anymore? I said to myself. Yes I didn't need him but I wanted him. Why is that too hard for him to understand? I asked him but he kept laughing. Two months earlier, Ryan had come to my house to collect Jimmy's books and other things, and he reported to Jimmy that it looked like there was a man living in my house and that I also looked like I had a man in my life because I looked healthier and happier than when I was with Jimmy. It's true, I was, and I am still happier than when I was living with Jimmy but he didn't want to hear that. My children are happy too. When Ryan came to collect the books, I had already replaced everything Jimmy took and I had also bought more new things for my house.

Jimmy told me on the phone that there was no way I could pay that big rent, pay bills, pay school and childcare fees, buy food and still be able to run my car without his help. He said that the only way I would be able to do all those things was if there was a man in my life! I reminded him that when we started dating, I was not homeless and I was not jobless but I was working, I was studying at the university and I had a house and a good car. I told him that he didn't meet me with another man and took me from that man to give me a better life, but that I was a single mother with no support and still managed my life well. He said that since I didn't 'need' him in my life anymore, let my new man continue to provide for me and he should also give to my children what he should have given them. He warned me to stay away from him and his new woman or else. He said that he wasn't going to tell me that he was in a relationship with another woman because whatever he was doing at the time was no longer any of my business but he just had to tell me to keep me and my children away. The woman he was talking about was not an ex-girlfriend but a new woman. My goodness, Jimmy has already disconnected himself from me and our children and he even has another woman! I said to myself. For how long had he been planning to move in with this new woman? How long had he known this woman for him to move in with her? Does that mean that I was right all along and he had been cheating on me with her even when I was pregnant with his baby? There I was, telling him how I was feeling, how lonely I was and updating him on our children's progress through messages and pictures and pleading with him to come back home, thinking that wherever he was, he was probably not happy. But he was actually happy and he had already moved on with another woman in less than six months since the birth of our baby! He could not even acknowledge that he had hurt me and he didn't even care about his children!

He knew that if I found out that he was in a relationship with another woman, I would be unhappy and I would blame him for moving on so quickly, so he had to accuse me of having another man in my life so that people or even our children would not blame him for moving on so quickly. He tried hard to find some loose ends in me so he could use them as an excuse for him moving on so quickly with another woman but he didn't find any loose ends. He continued to blame me for his poor choices and bad decisions up until September 2019 and that was when I stopped asking him to come back home. Because I knew then that he was never going to come back home and he was never going to have a committed relationship with our children, neither was he going to acknowledge that he has hurt us.

I see a lot of men here in Australia who are fighting a lot to make sure that they have access to their children at least once a week but Jimmy is willingly refusing to have access to his children and refusing to have anything to do with them! What did my children do to deserve this? They are innocent, why should they have to be punished for our mistakes? What happened between me and him was between me and him, why did he have to bring our children in and punish them? I begged him to punish me instead and leave my children out of it but he said nothing. I even came up with a suggestion that he could spend every second weekend with our children in his house but he refused. I told him that we didn't have to see each other and I didn't have to know his address but we could get someone to assess his house for safety and find someone to pick up our children from my house and take them to his house and then bring them back but he refused. He didn't agree with any suggestion I came up with and yet he didn't come up with any suggestion apart from telling me that he does not want to have anything to do with me and my children!

I have apologised to him so many times for things that I did and things that I didn't do but he has refused to forgive me. Even our older daughter has written him letters and Bible verses, begging him to forgive me and come back home but he has refused to even listen to our daughter. Every time our daughter has given him a letter or a Bible verse, he would read it and drop the paper on the floor or on the table and then he would walk away. My daughter is so hurt because of the way he has treated all of us. My daughters have asked him so many times to take them to his house but he has refused and will not tell them the reason why. If a child wrote me a letter, I would drop everything I was doing, read the letter, sit that child down and listen to what the child wanted to tell me, but people are different.

Even when he has knocked me and my daughters back so many times, we still have not given up on him. I have left the door open for him to come in any time to see the children. He had been transporting our children to and from school on and off, only one day a week. But I have had to stop him from transporting the kids to school and I have also taken his name off the school pick up list because he had sometimes picked the kids up once or twice in a term or sometimes he doesn't pick them up at all for the whole term. He told me in early July 2020 that the reason why he wasn't transporting our children to and from school regularly is because I am 'staying at home doing nothing' and that he sees no reason why he should go to work and then transport my children to school at the same time when I am here doing nothing. He also said that he would look after our children sometimes and have a committed relationship with them when I go back to work. I told him that I am not going to abandon my children when I return to work but I will schedule my work hours around school drop off and pick times. He said that now that I have told him that I will only be working during school hours, he is also going to schedule his work hours during school hours to enable him drop and pick up the girls three days a week when I go back to work. I told him that he should have done that and have a committed relationship with our children from the beginning regardless of whether I was working or not. What Jimmy said to me in July 2020 has cleared the air and has given me a clear understanding of the reason why he left. For Jimmy to live with me and my children, I have to be working and earning income. My children were also starting to feel anxious about seeing him. Many times they had asked me to go to school with them in their dad's car and to also pick them up together with him if he was picking them up. They said that they didn't feel comfortable being with him alone in the car anymore. He doesn't make spending time with our children during school holidays or on public holidays a priority but his job has always come first. And even if he doesn't see our children for a whole year, he will not miss them. I am done running after him to try and get him to have a relationship with our children. It's up to him now to find a way to make his relationship with his children work but he will never get back the years and the time he has wasted staying away from our children. In August

2018, I had a car accident and I didn't have a car for two months and during that time, Jimmy transported my children to and from school every day and he also took me to my personal appointments and shopping and he enjoyed doing it. He was even spending a lot of time with us and having dinner with us on most nights during that time but it didn't last. My children and I were very happy because we thought that he was going to come back home but as soon as I picked up my new car, he disappeared.

After he moved out, his family started to stalk me on social media, in the community and even in my own home. Every time I wrote something on Facebook, they would attack me by saying that I was writing about Jimmy or them and they would call me a 'bad and emotionally disturbed woman'. Even though what I had posted on Facebook had nothing to do with the South Sudanese community, the Ugandan community or with Jimmy's relatives, they would still attack me and hold grudges against me. If I post a picture of me and my children on Facebook, Abby Jimmy's niece would say that I am seeking attention. Abby told me on a number of occasions that my Facebook activity indicated that I was mentally ill and that I should be locked up in a mental health institution to get proper help. They also started to listen to the Christian radio that I always listen to, to find out if I would talk about Jimmy or their family on the radio. One day, Abby contacted me and told me that she had been hearing me on the Christian radio talking about relationship and family issues. She said that I was embarrassing myself on the radio for talking about my relationship with Jimmy and his relatives. She said that I was a 'loser' and that nobody was interested in my 'relationship fiasco'. She also said that I should go for mental health treatment and fix my brain and find another man and another family to manipulate but I should leave her uncle and his relatives alone. Every time I attend radio interviews on different radio stations in South Australia and whenever they read a story in the paper about my book and my journey to Australia, they would contact me to bully me by saying that I am a confused manipulator. Every time I go to community events and they are also there, they would come and sit at my table and at the tables next to me to keep people, especially men, away from me by using their intimidating body language.

In May 2018, two months after we moved into the community housing where we reside now, I organised a barbecue in the house for my daughter's second birthday and I invited Jimmy's relatives. A few weeks later, Abby started to turn up to my house unannounced to see if she could catch me with another man but she has never met another man in my house. Sometimes she would ring me to say that she was on her way to my house when she was actually already in my street sitting in her car. She rang me one time in 2019 to talk on the phone and I told her that I couldn't talk because I was getting myself ready for a community meeting in my house. She ended the call and came to my house to confirm if I was really hosting a meeting or if I was entertaining another man. She sat in with us and listened to what we were talking about at the meeting for an hour and then she left. On another occasion, she rang me to say that she was on her way to my house and I told her that we were at the shop, but she was already in my street. She waited until we came back home with our shopping. She thought that I had gone shopping with another man and she waited to see but there was no man in my car; only my kids and my support worker. She also parked her car in my street on some occasions, sat there for some time and then she left without coming into my house. I didn't know that she was sitting in her car in my street until she told me in 2019! She said that she had come from somewhere and that she had to stop there to rest or to talk on the phone and she didn't come to my house because she was in a hurry. I actually believe that she was on my street to spy on me. She lives thirty minutes away from my house but she was parking on my street most of the time in 2019! She had even become friends with my main support worker on Facebook and she started chatting with her, which I think was a way of getting my support worker to talk to her about me, but my support worker blocked her after I told her that she was Jimmy's niece.

Whenever Abby came to my house, she would sit on the couch and demand that my support workers serve her food. Abby wouldn't come to my house to help me but to eat and then leave. To me, that kind of behaviour doesn't seem normal and I don't know what she and her family really want from me. One minute I'm a bad woman, and one minute they are stalking me and trying to keep men away from me. If I am a bad woman, why are they still wasting their time to talk to me, to attack me, to stalk and to spy on me? I ask myself. Why can't they leave me alone and make good use of their time? Anyway, I have decided to ignore them, mind my own business and continue to write books, share my story and attend interviews because engaging with them is not going to be productive or helpful to me. I'm sure that very soon they will find something else to talk about and waste their precious time on.

Thirteen

THE AFTERMATH

I had one last thing left to do which was to accept that the problem I was facing was bigger than me but I wasn't going to give up just yet. I was prepared to approach the situation spiritually because I believed that only the power of prayer would change the situation. Whatever I was saying or doing at the time was not going to change anything and it was not going to bring Jimmy back. I said to myself, if only I had faith like prophet Elijah's in the Bible to call fire to come down from heaven through prayers and change a difficult situation in an instant (1 Kings 18), I would pray on my knees and God would change my own relationship situation. And so I started to pray and I prayed. I was hurting myself even more every time I sent a message to Jimmy or rang him and he didn't respond. Maybe prayers will help, I said to myself. I knew that my children needed me so I had to get myself together for me and for my children and stop worrying about Jimmy and his relatives but I didn't know how. Perhaps I should stop ringing or texting him but will that work? I asked myself.

How do you suddenly switch off loving someone, having strong feelings for someone and being emotionally connected to someone? For me, seeing him in my house and talking to him calmly, whether once or twice a month, helped me to remove my feelings and myself from him slowly, bit by bit, and eventually I was also able to remove him from my system. Writing this book and reading it over and over again has also helped me to completely remove him from my system. The first thing you need to do after a relationship breakdown is to work on your emotional struggles. Once you have moved on emotionally, you will easily be able to move on physically.

Some people say that starting to date again straight away after a relationship breakdown helps them to move on quickly. But I believe that this is just a physical moving on, not an emotional moving on. I also believe that moving on so quickly without properly resolving the issues from your previous relationship will mean that you will be carrying issues from one relationship to the next. And one day, the demons of your past will catch up with you and come back to bite you. If you are coming out of a long-term relationship, it is important that you be kind to yourself; give yourself enough time to grieve and heal. When it feels right to start dating again, then go for it. I tried dating in late 2019 and even kissed someone on two different occasions but as we were kissing, I remembered how Jimmy used to kiss me and everything stopped. I also went on two casual lunch dates with two men in late 2019 but I didn't go on second dates with them because I felt that I wasn't ready and dating at that time didn't feel right. I still felt like I was cheating on Jimmy even though he had already moved on with other women a long time ago. I was also always looking over my shoulder to see who was watching whenever I was out in public and chatting with another man. It was then that I realised that I truly and genuinely loved Jimmy so I needed time to properly heal.

Do I still love Jimmy? Yes I do. Do I still have feelings for Jimmy? No. As a Christian, would I take Jimmy back if he is to come back? I don't think so. He has rejected me for so long to the extent that I have had to disconnect myself from him emotionally and I don't think that I will be able to emotionally reconnect with him again. I believe that there is nothing he will ever do to mend the broken pieces of my heart now. He had a lot of opportunities and a lot of time to make things right but he didn't. Maybe someone else will mend my heart one day but not him. I tried online dating for four months but I ended up deactivating my online dating account because I didn't feel that it was the right thing to do. I'm sure there is a man out there for me and when the right time comes, he will reveal himself. Maybe my next book will be about my fairytale romance with the right God-chosen man and about my happily ever after. Watch this space.

The next stage of my emotional journey had already begun. The sleepless nights increased and my body started to feel weaker and heavier. When I was walking, I felt like I was dragging myself along. My eyes could not see properly. The world around me was closing in and it was becoming darker by the day. Some days were better than others but some days were worse. Things continued like that for a little while. At this stage, I became aware that I needed extra time to complete a simple task that I would normally complete in five or ten minutes, for example having a shower, doing the dishes and even bathing my baby. I tried to be normal around my children and still smiled a lot and played with them but my five-year-old daughter sensed that I wasn't happy. My poor five-year-old daughter was caught up in the middle of it all. Organising transport for her to and from school at the last minute until I was able to drive again was a bit of a hassle but we got there in the end.

She watched me struggling and juggling everything and then one day, she dropped a bombshell. She had tried to talk to her dad without success — along with the letters and Bible verses to him, she had asked him to come back home on the phone on a number of occasions — and now she said, 'Mummy, can you please talk to my school and tell them that I am not coming back to school anymore?'

'Why?' I asked.

'Because you are doing all the hard work alone without any help yet you have bad legs,' she said.

'Daddy should come back home and take care of you because you are taking care of me and my baby sister. I will help you with bringing things closer to you and by putting the dirty nappies in the bin so you don't have to do a lot of walking that will make you feel so tired by the end of the day,' she added. 'I cannot sit by and watch you struggle trying to organise people here and there to drop me to school and back home every day when you should be using that time doing something. The only solution is for me to stay home,' she concluded!

She had also asked me to find a lawyer months earlier so that the lawyer could help bring daddy back home.

Hearing her say all those things hit me really hard and my heart sank. How do you tell a five-year-old that everything is going to be okay when she can see that you are struggling and when she can see the sadness in your eyes? I decided from that time on that I was going to stop putting my daughter through that emotional stress and be there for her and her little sister instead of her being there for me. So I told her that there would be no need for her to stay at home because mummy was going to start driving again in four days. Even though I was not yet medically cleared to drive because of the caesarean wound, I reassured her that everything was going to be okay.

I had to start driving my daughter to and from school with the unhealed caesarean wound. My friend Eleanor threatened to call the police if I continued to drive before I was medically cleared. Eleanor decided that even though she lived forty-five minutes away from my house, she would drive my daughter to and from school. She didn't care if she had to wake up at 5am every morning to get her children ready and then drive to my house to pick up my daughter and go to school. She also didn't care if they had to go to school late every day because of a long-distance drive to stop me from hurting my children and myself if anything happened while I was driving. She could not stand by and watch me hurt myself and my beautiful daughters. So Eleanor started transporting my daughter to and from school and another mother at school also put her hand up to help until I was finally medically cleared to drive again after my caesarean wound was healed.

Before my daughter said what she did, she had had a telephone conversation with her dad which didn't end well. She texted him first to ask him to answer her call and so he did answer when she rang. By that time, he was no longer answering my calls which is why my daughter texted him first. She asked her dad if he still loved her, her sister and her mummy, and he said yes. She then asked him why he didn't want to live with us anymore and he told her to ask me why he was not living with us anymore. 'No, I don't want to ask my mother, I am talking to you right now so you tell me,' she said. There was a sound of dead silence for a few minutes and my daughter quoted a Bible verse for her dad which stated that, 'You should be tolerant, persevere and forgive one another in all circumstances' (Colossians 3:13). She had learnt these from Sunday School a week earlier.

She pleaded with her dad to forgive me for her and her sister's sake and for him to return home but he didn't give her the answer she was looking for, instead he terminated the call. The phone went silent and she couldn't hear him anymore. 'Mummy he hung up on me,' she said, while crying. We hugged, we prayed together and then she went to play with her sister.

It was heartbreaking to see my daughter in that situation. One evening after putting my children to bed, I closed all the doors and I went back to the lounge. I picked up my iPad and I downloaded the song 'It is Well with my Soul'. I played the song over and over again and I sang along while crying and praying. I cannot remember how long I sang that song for but I do remember that my face and my chest were covered in tears and sweat. I went to bed afterwards and woke up in the morning to a very bright house again. The clouds had gone, my eyes could see properly and my body was lighter again. Everything had gone back to normal and I haven't looked back since.

This happened after many nights of crying and praying. On another occasion, I had fallen asleep on the couch after a day of fasting, lots of crying and prayers. To be honest, I don't remember how long I prayed for that night. I think I might have passed out or maybe God heard my cry and he made me go to sleep on the couch. I woke up at 1am feeling very cold and I panicked when I realised that I was sleeping on the couch and my baby was in the room all by herself. I rushed into my bedroom where my baby was sleeping and found my baby was sound asleep; I went to my five-year-old daughter's bedroom and she was also sleeping. I changed my baby's nappy, gave her a bottle and put her back to bed. This was the first time my baby slept until morning. By this time my breast milk had dried up and she was relying more on the bottle. The nights that followed she slept through without crying. We had found our new normal.

In January 2017, eight months after my daughter was born, we moved back to our two-bedroom public housing property in Black Forest that we lived in before we moved in with Jimmy. The house was smaller and more affordable than the private rental property but it was too small for the three of us so we had to move again in February 2018. This time, we moved into an affordable three-bedroom community housing with a big backyard, which is exactly what my children and I needed.

Before we moved out of Black Forest, a neighbour

threatened me with a knife, which kind of helped speed up our transfer. I rang the police and within five minutes there were more than eight police cars and more than twenty heavily armed police officers plus detectives and paramedics on the street, with four guarding my back and front doors holding high-powered rifles in their hands. There was a five-hour standoff between the police and the neighbour and he was eventually tasered and arrested. He also threatened the police with the knife and then he locked himself in his house. The police had to break into his house through the window to taser and arrest him when they realised that he was no longer safe in his own house. It was exactly like a scene in the movies but I am glad that nobody was physically hurt. I do believe that God allows certain situations to happen for a reason. Waking up to my children every morning kept me motivated and going. When I look into my children's eyes, I see hope, I see peace, I see love, I see purpose, I see contentment and I see a sense of belonging.

In March 2017, after we had moved into the small house, my phone rang. It was a new number and I answered, only to find Jimmy on the phone. My baby was ten months old at the time. When he rang me from a new number, I went quiet for some time thinking whether I should listen to what he had to say, whether I should talk to him or simply end the call but I decided to listen. He said that when he had left my house in June 2016, he was only going to clear his head for a few weeks and that he would have returned home, but because I didn't go after him to ask him for money and also the fact that I was doing well without him meant that I did not need him in my life anymore, that's why he didn't come back home. He also told me that if I needed help with looking after my children so I could have time to myself or go back to work that I should ask Sandy to babysit them. He said that he couldn't help me because he was working full time. I thanked him for his call and told him that I was busy and that I did not want to talk to him as he thought everything was still my fault. I terminated the call and continued doing what I was doing. I later rang Sandy and asked her to help me with babysitting but she asked me to pay her upfront. She said that if I was not able to pay her, I should go to Centrelink and apply for grandparents' payments to pay her as my children's grandmother! I thanked her and I never contacted her about babysitting my children again.

I reported back to Jimmy what Sandy had told me and he went quiet. Jimmy had changed his tone this time. He was no longer sounding happy on the phone and he wasn't laughing anymore! Why did he call me and tell me that? Did he want to come back home? Did he have a fight with his new woman? Did he break up with her? What was going on? Why did he clear our house and take all our things if he was only going to clear his head? I asked myself all these questions. But wait a minute, could I trust him again? No, I said to myself, I am not going back there again. It has taken me a very long time and a lot of work to get to where I am now. I am not going to open that chapter so I can be hurt again, I told myself. He has always contacted me and spoken to me in a kind way if he is single again or if he is fighting with his girlfriends but as soon as they reconcile or he meets another woman, he would forget about me. He thinks that he can walk in and out of my life any time he wants because he knows that I love him and that I will always sit there and wait for him to become available. But this time, he is not going to treat me like the other woman again. If he is fighting or if he is broken up with his girlfriends, he should go and find comfort somewhere else but not with me, I said to myself.

When he left, people said that I was finished, others said that I deserved it because I treated him very poorly! Others wasted a lot of time gossiping and spreading rumours about me and others, including two of his nieces, called me names. Others said things like, 'now that he is gone, let us see how she is going to manage paying the rent, bills and looking after the children without him'! But as months went by and there were no court proceedings to obtain child support, and I was not admitted to a mental health institution, people began to change their story. And they started to say that I kicked him out of my house because he treated me badly. All of a sudden, it had become a case of me kicking him out of my house because of how badly he treated me! Why are people always looking for the wrong or the worst in others? Why can't we build ourselves and others up instead? I asked myself.

Even though I still have not told my children what really happened between me and their dad, my children now resent him and they have started saying things like, when they are married and they have children of their own, they will not allow Jimmy to come anywhere near their children. 'How could he leave us when we were small and then he would want to be in our children's life?' they asked me. My children don't miss him anymore but they are happy to see him whenever he comes to our house, even if it's only for two minutes. They are also happy to talk to him on the phone just like any of our friends but not like their dad even though they still call him Dad. If he comes and stays in my house for longer than five minutes, which is what he usually does, my children will start asking why he is not leaving or when he is going to leave.

Despite everything Jimmy has done to me and my children and despite being in and out of my children's lives, I still allow him to talk to my children and to visit them when he can and I have also continued to host dinners and lunches in my house and invite his relatives when I can. I also believe that one day, when the hovering dark cloud is gone, he will commit to having a relationship with our children and I hope it will not be too late. I don't want my children to grow up without a dad like I did and I do hope that, soon, he will start to realise what he is missing out on and start being a dad to my children rather than being a visitor in our house. I hope that my patience will pay off one day. My children want to go to his house and see where he lives but he has refused to take them to his house. They have asked him so many times if they could go to his house but his answer has always been 'no' or 'maybe one day'. My children should not be asking him to take them to his house but he should willingly take them to his house and spend time with them on weekends, during school holidays and on public holidays. That's what I would do if I was in his position and I would fight for my children to be in my life but I am not him.

Fourteen

DESTINY, MY FIRST DAUGHTER

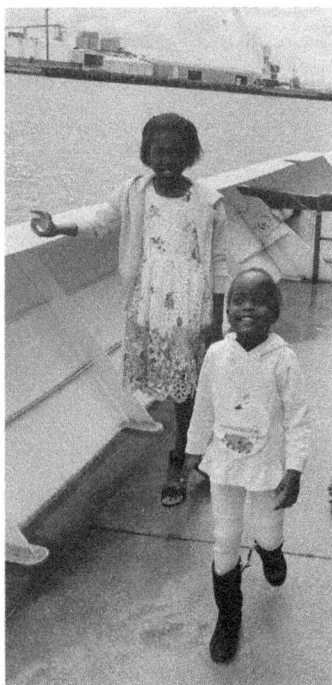

Esther's daughters, Destiny and Dorcas,
on the Dolphin Cruise in Port Adelaide

My three daughters are Destiny, Hannah and Dorcas. I love being a mother and I could never trade the feeling of being a mum with anything else in my life. When I was young, I had always prayed to be a mum but what I didn't know was that I was going to be a single mother. My ten-year journey of being a mother and a single mother has been a very long one. There have been a lot of highs and lows, a lot of challenges, lots of laughter and there has also been a lot of tears and joy and I couldn't have done it any other way. The only thing I have missed is not being able to carry my babies on my back, just like how the South Sudanese mothers do, because of my weak legs and lower back. But the good news is that I have always been there for my daughters from the start and on every single day of their lives. Because I am not able to carry my daughters when walking, I used the bassinet and the pram / baby pusher to wheel them from the bedroom to the bathroom and then to the lounge and back to the bedroom in the night. I parked the bassinet or the pram closer to the couch so it was easier for me to transfer my baby to the couch when she was crying. I fed them and changed their nappies on the couch during the day. In the night, I wheeled them next to my bed, took them out of the bassinet or pram, fed them and changed their nappies on my bed or changed their nappies on their baby bed. As they grew older and started walking, I asked them to walk to the lounge in the morning so I could change their nappies there. I toilet trained my babies early so by the time they were two years old, they would be out of nappies. Both my daughters came off nappies at age two and they started going to the toilet in the night from three years old.

Pushing my children in the bassinet and pram helped me with my mobility but it didn't stop my falls. I fell once in the house when I was pushing Destiny in the pram. The pram went running and it came to a sudden stop on a chair but Destiny was okay. I fell once at Destiny's school when I was pushing Dorcas in the pram. I hung onto the pram so tight as I went down so that the pram wouldn't go flying and falling. Instead, the pram fell backwards but Dorcas was okay. She was secure in the pram and she didn't hit her head on the ground. I was shaken and I started to cry, thinking I had hurt Dorcas, but a student in the playground saw me and came to me to give me comfort. Nothing about Dorcas changed after she woke up from her sleep, she was still her normal self. But I took her to the doctor anyway to make sure she was okay and, yes, she was okay and she didn't need any scan.

When Destiny was born we lived in a small two-bedroom house with no bath until she was four years old and we moved into a house with a big bath with Jimmy. I used to bathe her in a portable bath when she was a baby but when she started walking and was stable on her feet, I started to put her under the shower to wash her there.

Slowly but surely, she stated to bathe and shower herself. It has been tough being a single mother with a disability but I have found a way that works for me to manage myself and my children.

Destiny sitting on her bike in the backyard at home

Esther's daughter, Destiny, at her mum's first
book launch in Adelaide in June 2019

Destiny is a sweet, kind, smart, intelligent, sensitive and beautiful little darling, but she is also loud. She knew from when she was one and a half years old that something was wrong with my legs and she used to kiss my feet and say sorry to my feet. She asked me why I walked differently to her and I told her that when I was four years old, I had a fever and woke up with a paralysed body and that's why I walk like this.

Destiny has always been cautious and protective of me, and she is not a risk-taker like her little sister, Dorcas. Dorcas is more protective of me now than Destiny was when she was Dorcas's age. If she climbs up on something and falls or hurts herself, she will not climb up on that thing again. My pregnancy with Destiny made me feel like I had reached my destiny by becoming a mother and that's why I named her Destiny.

Some people think that if you have a disability that you are cursed and therefore not blessed but that is not true. People can have a disability and can still be blessed with a lot of things in their lives. In my young lifetime, God has blessed me with education, knowledge, wisdom and understanding, and good health. God blessed me with a humanitarian visa to come to Australia, God blessed me with accommodation and, above all, God has blessed me with three beautiful daughters. When I was young, before I became pregnant with my first child, people had a lot of theories about me. Some said that I would not be able to have children because of my disability, and others told me that I would not be able to carry a pregnancy to full term because of my scoliosis, my weak back and weak legs. Others told me that even if I were able to have children, I would not be able to look after them because of my disability! I looked at them and I said, watch me! People told me to work hard and save enough money to adopt a child, but I told them that I would have children of my own, and now I am a proud mother of two beautiful daughters. Against all odds, I have had three pregnancies; unfortunately, my second daughter was born premature in June 2015 and she died a few minutes after she was born. I want to clarify: the premature birth of my daughter had nothing to do with the fact that I have a disability. God had his own reasons for taking her away from me so early in her life.

In early March 2010, I found out that I was pregnant with my first baby and I was thrilled. I should have been worried that I was going to be a single mother with a disability and with no family support but I wasn't. Instead, I was very happy because I was ready to be a mum. Since I was young in Uganda, I had always prayed for children and I wanted to have three children but I didn't know that 2010 was the year I was going to have my first baby. In my mind I was like, I will prove to everyone that even when you have a disability, you can still have children. I might not have been ready physically, but I was very ready emotionally and psychologically. Once you are ready to do something psychologically and emotionally, your physical body will automatically agree to it and become ready as well. Which is why people should pay closer attention to their inner body and ask the question, where am I in life psychologically? Am I emotionally ready for this and that? Even though I was emotionally ready to be a mother, I still had to get myself ready psychologically and physically for whatever lay ahead in the world of single parenthood. I prayed to God to give me strength, energy and good health to be able to look after my daughter as a single mother and God did. I started telling myself that I could do this and, day by day, I saw myself going from strength to strength and by the time my daughter was born, I had become a stronger woman compared to what I was before. I surprised myself. The birth of my first child not only changed my life physically and financially but it also changed me as a person emotionally. I found myself crying over little things after she was born and I didn't know why. My friends told me that hormones made me cry over little things. It was then I realised that it was not only me that I had to think about but I also had to think about my beautiful daughter too.

After I realised that I missed my period in February 2010, I went to my local Coles to buy a pregnancy testing kit, came home to test myself and, sure enough, it was positive. I threw the testing kit away, did a little quirky dance and dropped on my knees to thank God for the gift of life. I then rang my GP and booked an appointment for the next day. I had another urine test at the GP and the test confirmed that I was pregnant. I had a blood test done too and the blood test also confirmed that I was pregnant. My GP organised an ultrasound for me and the ultrasound confirmed that I was six weeks pregnant! She also referred me to the Women's and Children's Hospital (WCH) in Adelaide for my antenatal visits and the visits started.

Oh wow, six weeks pregnant already and I didn't even know it! I didn't feel any different and everything still felt the same. I used to hear women say that when you are pregnant, you will know from week four because by that time some women will start to have morning sickness, including vomiting, loss of appetite or increased appetite, and certain things will start to smell bad to them. I was totally fine and I was still eating everything. Nothing was smelling bad to me and I had not started having cravings but if I had paid close attention to my physical body, I would have realised that my breasts were starting to look bigger and felt firmer than usual. A few weeks after attending my first antenatal appointment at the WCH, I started to feel hungrier than usual, I was feeling nauseous but I didn't vomit for the whole of my pregnancy and my whole body had also started to become bigger, especially my belly and breasts. I was three months pregnant when I had my first antenatal appointment. I started to sleep more and I had also started to crave certain foods that I would normally avoid, such as prawns, cheese and crackers. Certain things, including my body lotion, perfume and meat, had also started to smell bad. I stopped eating meat until I was six months pregnant. Instead, I ate a lot of fish, vegetables and fruit. I also cooked with a lot of chilli which was unusual. I could not eat anything without chilli. Every time I went to the shops, I would pick up what I had gone there to buy and leave the shop as quickly as I could because I didn't like the smell of certain things in the shops anymore.

After my GP confirmed that I was pregnant, I rang

Harry to tell him but he told me that he did not want to have anything to do with my pregnancy. That he did not want to have a child with a mother with a disability. I wasn't surprised because I had already known that this was going to happen after he went to Africa and married a woman with no disability (see Chapter 6). Even though I knew that I was capable of raising my daughter single-handedly, I still told him because I wanted Harry to be in my daughter's life and have a relationship with her but he didn't want to be involved. She is his first child and the only child he had at the time but he didn't want to hear of it. I am sure that if I didn't have a disability, he would have thrown a big party to celebrate the good news of the pregnancy but because I have a disability, he disappeared. I was hoping that the pregnancy news would change his mind and that he could change his lifestyle after the baby was born and would try to be involved but he didn't change his mind. Instead, he went to Africa and made his wife there pregnant to prove to me that he meant business. He is now happily married with two children from that woman. He doesn't even ring to ask how my daughter is going.

I was working with Disability SA as a service coordinator and I was also studying my Master's degree in Mediation and Conflict Resolution at the time I was pregnant with Destiny. But when I was five months pregnant, I deferred my studies to 2011 and I stopped working when I was seven months pregnant, a few weeks after my bleeding episode (described in Chapter 15). When Destiny was ten months old in 2011, I returned to work and I also resumed my studies.

When I was pregnant with my first daughter, I had people lined up waiting to take my baby away from me because they thought that I would not be able to look after her, but I proved to everyone that I am capable of looking after my children regardless of my disability. I am happy to say that I am still able to raise my two beautiful girls alone without any help from anybody. I remember laying down on the hospital bed two weeks after my first child was born, wondering if I would ever be allowed to take her home with me, as the doctors were not in any hurry to discharge me. Two weeks later, I was discharged to go home with my daughter and with in-home support services in place, but the occupational therapist from the WCH followed me home. He came fifteen minutes after I had arrived home to determine whether my house was a suitable environment for my baby to live in.

They had assumed that because I was a young, first-time single mother with a disability from a refugee back-ground, I couldn't afford a clean and decent house to raise my daughter in. The occupational therapist was blown away when he saw that I had my house set up ready for my baby. I had a bassinet, a bed and other baby gear all in place before I went to the hospital to have her. I gathered that the occupational therapist was prepared to make arrangements to take my baby away from me there and then, but because I was able to prove to him that disability is not inability, I got to keep my baby. If you put your mind to something, your determination will help you to achieve your goals in life, regardless of your disability, mental illness, medical condition or any other limitation. I believe that disability is not inability; therefore, people with disabilities should be given the chance to explore new opportunities that will enable them to reach their full potential, whatever that may look like for them. Whether having children, obtaining education or having a job, they should be supported to achieve their goals. I believe that with a positive mindset, and with assistance, people with disabilities can function well when they are given the right kind of support.

Fifteen

HANNAH, MY SECOND DAUGHTER

In February 2015, I found out that I was pregnant with my second child, Jimmy's first child, and I couldn't have been happier. My pregnancy with Hannah made me feel like I had finally arrived home and that's why I named her Hannah because it had been a very long journey coming home with lots of prayers along the way. I felt that God had finally answered my prayers and that not only did he bring me home from my long journey, but he had also provided me with a home and a family.

I felt that something was not right from the minute Hannah was conceived. I felt intense pain in my tummy from the night she was conceived and the pain persisted for three weeks. I thought that the pain was going to go away but it instead became worse three weeks into my pregnancy. By week four, the pain had stopped and everything seemed normal for a little while but by week nine, things took a turn for the worse when I started bleeding. Every time I went to the toilet, there was a little blood on the toilet paper. The first time it happened, I noticed the blood only when I got up to flush the toilet. From this time on, I started monitoring how much blood there was and how often, but there was not much blood to cause alarm until I was fourteen weeks pregnant. At twelve weeks, I told the radiographer at my twelve-week scan that I had been bleeding and she told me after the scan that everything looked normal. There was nothing unusual in the images but she told me to ring the hospital and let them know. I rang the hospital and spoke to a midwife but they couldn't see me any sooner than the antenatal appointment I had already booked for the next two weeks. There were only spots on the toilet paper here and there and nothing in my knickers at this stage, but by the time I saw the doctor at the WCH, I had started spotting in my underwear.

A few days earlier, Jimmy and I had gone to his sister Sandy's house for dinner and to tell them that we were pregnant. There was a lot of joy, screaming and tears of happiness after Jimmy's relatives saw the scan images of our unborn baby. To them, this was a long time coming and a cause for celebration. Everyone at Sandy's house was touching and rubbing my tummy and there was a lot of singing and dancing, cooking and then we ate a late dinner. They rang all their relatives in Australia and in Africa to tell them the news and those relatives in Adelaide who were able to come to Sandy's house that night did come, while those who were not able to come rang to congratulate us and Jimmy and I spoke with them on the phone. Unfortunately, I started bleeding that same evening at Sandy's house to the extent that I had to go to the toilet more than once to wear and change a pad. I carried pads with me in my handbag everywhere I went because the midwife from the WCH had told me to wear pads to capture how much blood was coming out to help them with their assessment of my situation. I couldn't tell anyone that evening, not even Jimmy, that I was bleeding. I didn't want to ruin the evening for everyone. I was scared but I honestly didn't think that I was going to lose my baby. I thought that the bleeding was going to pass and everything was going to be okay.

Some women had told me before that they had had big bleeds during their early stages of pregnancy but the bleeding stopped and they went on to have healthy babies. Another woman told me that she bled for the whole pregnancy with all her five children and she had very healthy babies. She also said that she had to wear pads throughout her pregnancy. When I was six months pregnant with Destiny, I had a big bleed one day a few minutes after returning home from work. When I went to the toilet, I saw the toilet bowl was filled with blood but that was it. I didn't bleed again and Destiny was born healthy. I rang the ambulance and I stayed in the hospital for four days but I was discharged and nothing else happened. I thought that it was going to be the same thing with Hannah, but this time something was different. Jimmy and I got back home from Sandy's house at midnight and by this time the bleeding had stopped. The bleeding had lasted for about an hour at Sandy's house. By the time we got home, I was dry. This was the first time I had had a big bleed in a short period of time and I didn't have tummy cramps, tummy pain or a blood clot. We had a good night's sleep but I woke up at 3am, went to the toilet and there was another big bleed and this time the bleeding did not stop. I rang the midwife, who asked if I had blood clots and I said no and she also asked if I had tummy cramps and tummy pain and I said no. So she told me to go to emergency in the morning. There was no doctor there that night who could help me as they were dealing with more urgent issues at the time. I went to emergency in the morning but I was sent back home after the assessment without any treatment. I had scans done and the scans indicated that the baby was growing well and was getting bigger. The doctors couldn't work out where the bleeding was coming from.

Four weeks later, I went to the hospital in an ambulance one night after waking up with a soaked pad. I went to the toilet and felt something big fall into the toilet. I was terrified and thought that my baby had fallen into the toilet but it was a blood clot as big as a golf ball. That was the first time I had had a blood clot since I started bleeding. I was eighteen weeks pregnant. I stayed in the hospital for a week and was discharged. By eighteen weeks, I had had ten scans and an X-ray but the doctors still couldn't find out what was wrong with my pregnancy, and my baby was growing bigger and bigger. All they said was that there was a big black spot at the back of my placenta and they thought that was where the bleeding was coming from. By twenty-one weeks, I had gone to the hospital in an ambulance and I had stayed at the hospital four times.

The bleeding didn't seem to have affected the baby until twenty-one weeks when the doctors discovered that the baby was feeding on poisoned blood. The baby, though, was healthy and was growing bigger and bigger every day. By this time, three-quarters of my placenta had gone black and I was having more regular discharge of blood clots. Some of them were as big as a golf ball and some of them were small. The baby was still growing, kicking and looking very healthy on the scans and X-ray. I was referred to a specialist within the WCH who said that I was the fourth woman who had presented to the hospital with the same condition and that they were still trying to figure out what was causing it and how to name the condition. At twenty-one weeks and two days, my uterus gave way and everything in it, including the baby, came out. The baby came out with a heartbeat but her tiny heart stopped beating two to three minutes later. Even though her tiny lungs were not fully grown and even without a breathing aid, she took a few breaths before she gave up. My baby was a fighter and I'm sure that she would have been a strong woman, even stronger than I am, if she had survived. She fought right to the end. I am sure that if she had come out at twenty-two or twenty-three weeks, she would have survived given how strong she was.

I lost my baby at 6am after twelve whole hours of labour pain and agony. By the time my baby came out, I had no energy to cry or do anything. Jimmy's relatives thought that it was rather strange that I didn't cry at the hospital. I had been crying from the first day I went to the hospital in an ambulance and stayed there for a week until the night I was in labour. But after we came home that night, I couldn't contain my emotions. Jimmy and I hugged and I cried and cried and cried. Jimmy hugged and cuddled me and he remained strong for me. He didn't cry in my presence but I was informed by friends later that he mourned our baby for a long time and, to be honest, I don't think that he has ever recovered from the loss of our baby. The loss of our baby brought us closer than ever before and I didn't think that he was ever going to leave me. By 9am, there were more than twenty people in my birthing room crying and others were talking but I didn't cry. I was exhausted, hungry and I needed to sleep but I couldn't sleep with the noise in the room. We stayed there until 4pm and we went home to Sandy's house, where there were more people waiting for us and crying. Even then I didn't eat anything until 10pm when my body began to shake. None of the people who came to the hospital that day brought tea, porridge or food for me. I was starving, exhausted and I needed to eat something fast before I collapsed but there was no food and I had to wait until 10pm to eat dinner in Sandy's house. The last time I had eaten was 2pm the day before. We left Sandy's house immediately after eating a late dinner and we went back home to my place where I opened up and burst into tears.

I was criticised by Jimmy's relatives for not breaking down and crying with the others in the hospital room after the loss of my baby. Two days later, we buried my baby and we went back to Sandy's house for prayers and dinner. On our way to Sandy's house, I asked Jimmy, who was driving us, to go to KFC drive-through and buy some food for me, which he did but I was still hungry ten minutes later, even after eating two original twisters from KFC. But wait a minute, why am I thinking about food when I should be crying? I asked myself. I was thinking of food because I hadn't eaten since 2pm the day before and I was not only starving but my body was weak and shaky too. It was from this time that I started eating big meals and having sweet drinks (Hungry Jack's sundaes) all the time, which was actually my own way of dealing with the loss of my baby. It's only now that I realise I was stress eating back then. Between July 2015 and July 2016, my eating habits had changed and I was starting to find comfort in food so I ate a lot of food and drank a lot of sweet drinks. I was also eating chocolates in between meals, which was a new thing for me.

Before long, I had gained a lot of weight and I was starting to look like I was six months pregnant, which later resulted in gestational diabetes when I was seven months pregnant with Dorcas, my third daughter. I weighed 68 kilograms when I found out that I was pregnant with Dorcas and within five months, my weight had gone up to 75 kilograms and then I weighed 82 kilograms when Dorcas was born. Six months after Dorcas was born, I weighted 88 kilograms. In early 2018, I went back to under 70 kilograms but in August that year I started taking medication for my knee pain and the medication made me gain over 10 kilograms in less than two years. In January 2020 I had the cortisone injection in my knee which enabled me to go off medication. By March 2020, I was under 75 kilograms. I think I'm heading in the right direction weight wise. Even though I have a physical disability, I have always been fit and I had maintained a weight of 66 kilograms for about ten years after arriving in Australia.

A few days after we buried my daughter, I started to

feel guilty. I felt like I had let Jimmy down by not being able to give him a healthy living child and I started to contemplate leaving him so he could marry another woman and have children with her. I didn't know that Jimmy was also thinking the exact same thing. Jimmy was disappointed that I lost his first child so he planned to leave and not to have any more children with me because he thought that I would lose the next pregnancies. It's terrible to be blamed for the loss of a child especially when I didn't do anything wrong. I couldn't make sense of the situation. People were telling me to forget my deceased daughter because I already had a healthy older daughter. And others were saying that maybe God knew that if my middle daughter had lived, that she would have a disability and that's why God took her away from me to remove the burden of me raising a child with a disability! These are not the kind of things that someone should say to a grieving mother. Yes, I have a healthy older daughter but she cannot replace her dead sister, I said to them. It is not only my daughter that died and was buried at the cemetery but part of me died and was buried with her too. Why is this too hard for people to understand? I asked myself while crying. One afternoon when Jimmy was at work, my daughter Destiny and I drove to Glenelg at 4pm and then to Colonnades shopping centre in Adelaide at 7pm but we couldn't find our way back home sooner. We got home at 9:40pm, I gave her dinner and she went to bed just before Jimmy got back home from work. When I got behind the wheel of the car that afternoon, my plan was to disappear and not see Jimmy again but when I saw my daughter sitting in her booster seat very cutely in the back of the car, I decided to just drive around the neighbourhood to clear my head and then return home. I went too far and ended up in the Colonnades, a place I had never been before, and I didn't have a GPS to direct me back home. I panicked but I was able to get back home. I was lonely after the loss of my daughter. Jimmy's relatives had stopped communicating or visiting me. It was like they were blaming me for the loss of my baby and, yes, they were. The only comfort I received was from Jimmy when he was at home but when he was not home, I found comfort in food. My Church, my sister and a couple of women in my community visited and messaged me once in a while to check on how I was doing but I was mostly lonely. Despite all that happened, I came out of that situation very strong. I became stronger after I found out that I was pregnant with my third child, Dorcas.

Sixteen

DORCAS, MY THIRD DAUGHTER

Esther's daughter, Dorcas, went to buy a
vacuum cleaner at Godfreys in Adelaide with her mum

Dorcas is my third daughter. She is bubbly, strong willed, loud, out there and a risk-taker. She loves to sing, dance and she is an entertainer. My children and I love singing and dancing all the time especially in the mornings when we are getting ready for school and when we are in the shower. Sometimes we compete to see who sings and dances the best but I always win; don't tell them. Which is why Dorcas has continued singing and dancing all the time even when Destiny and I are not singing. Dorcas never gives up. She is always running into things and hurting herself but she will do it over and over again. If she falls off something and hurts herself, she will cry for a few seconds and then she will climb back up on that object. She is starting to stand on her head at the moment. So cute, I think. Maybe she is going to be my little gymnast.

My pregnancy with Dorcas made me feel like I finally had a sense of belonging because this time I felt complete. I had Destiny, I had a good job that I thought I would return to after Dorcas was born and, above all, I had a husband, Jimmy, who was living with me in the same house, which was what I had always prayed for. I was going to name Dorcas Rebekah or Debra from the Bible or even Margaret, given that she was born two days after my mother Margaret passed away, but I named her Dorcas because this name fits her well, as she was conceived three months after we lost her big sister Hannah. To me, it was like Hannah was back. Don't get me wrong, Dorcas is not in any form a replacement for Hannah but she reminds me a lot of Hannah and she makes me keep Hannah's memory alive every day.

Dorcas was born with a congenital pulmonary airway malformation (CPAM). CPAM is a malformation of the tissue that supplies blood and air into the lung. This is a common non-life-threatening condition found in newborn babies or infants. In some children, the tissue grows into a lump which then pushes the lung out of place and it can become life threatening when this happens because the lung will not be able to function properly. The good news is that CPAM can be fixed through surgery. The lump needs to be cut out to leave plenty of space for the lung to breathe. If the baby catches a cough, cold, flu or pneumonia, this may become life threatening. In some children, the CPAM disappears as the child grows and so they do not need surgery. In other children, like my daughter, the CPAM neither grows nor disappears, which also does not require surgery.

Dorcas's conception couldn't have come at a better time. I was working with the Young Women's Christian Association in Adelaide as a project coordinator when I found out that I was pregnant with Dorcas, four months after I lost Hannah. I was five weeks pregnant when I found out. I wasted no time and rang my GP straight away and went to see her the following day to confirm my pregnancy test. My GP referred me to the Women's and

Children's Hospital for further pregnancy care. I received a call from the WCH a few days later advising me to go and see a doctor at the hospital immediately. I saw the doctor a few days later and he referred me to the WCH's Maternal Fetal Medicine Service (MFMS) for high-needs pregnancy care.

The MFMS is, according to the WCH website, 'a specialised multidisciplinary service with a diverse medical and midwifery faculty providing expert diagnosis, ongoing surveillance and discerning management for women whose pregnancies are significantly complicated by maternal and/or fetal conditions'. My pregnancy with Dorcas was labelled a 'high-risk pregnancy', which was not the news I wanted to hear. Having a high-risk pregnancy meant that I would be seen by specialists and going to the hospital once a fortnight. Worst case scenario, I would be going to the hospital once a week until my baby was born. This would also mean hospital stays for most of my pregnancy to monitor my baby until she was born. The doctors I saw at the MFMS told me that there was a greater chance that I would lose my baby again given my history! I didn't know what they meant by 'given your history'. I have never had any miscarriages and my middle child was born alive but she was too young to breathe on her own or with support because her tiny lungs had not developed properly. I wasn't given any diagnosis of any kind before and after I lost my middle child. Why are the doctors telling me that there is a greater chance of me losing my baby again? I asked myself. The doctors didn't give me any hope whatsoever but they instead told me to prepare for the worst.

I left the hospital very strong, armed and ready for a fight. I wasn't going to fight the doctors or anyone but I equipped myself ready to fight the devil, who was robbing me of my happiness as a mother. I went home and locked myself in my room and I began to pray. I said God, the doctors have given me their verdict, what is your own verdict God. I told God that he created that little human in my womb for a reason and I wanted to see his Will done in my life and in the life of my unborn baby. I told God that my uterus was not going to give way this time but my baby was going to grow and would come out when the time was right in Jesus's name. I told God that I had seen a lot of deaths and I had lost so much in my life and that I had come to Australia for a better life, not to bury my children. If I keep burying my children, who is going to bury me? I asked and I wept. In South Sudanese culture, children are to look after their parents in their old age and are to bury them after they have passed on. I already had Destiny, my older daughter, but she needed a sibling to share the responsibility of looking after me and to support each other. After I had finished talking to God, I started rebuking the devil and I commanded the devil to leave my body, my life, my house and my family in Jesus's name. A few minutes later, I came out of my room and I went to pick up my daughter from childcare.

I had three visits to the MFMS and I was sent back to the normal outpatient maternity clinic. I was fourteen weeks pregnant by that time. The doctors said that my pregnancy was no longer high risk, which I was relieved to hear. They couldn't explain to me why my pregnancy was no longer high risk but I think I knew why. It was because God was at work. I had a once-off, very small vaginal discharge when I was five weeks pregnant but the doctors said it was normal. The discharge was not completely red, which the doctors said was a good sign. They said that some women get vaginal discharge at five weeks as a result of the placenta planting itself firmly onto the uterus wall.

At eighteen weeks, I had an ultrasound and the images indicated a dark grey spot in my baby's right lung. Here we go again, I said to myself while trembling. It was investigated further and the doctors found that it was a congenital pulmonary airway malformation. They reassured me that the CPAM condition was not going to kill my baby but that she might require surgery immediately after she was born. This time I didn't panic and I said that the devil was a liar. I continued going to the hospital for monitoring until the baby was born. She was born three weeks early but healthy. I had a caesarean section booked at forty weeks but I went into labour at thirty-seven weeks and five days. My caesarean section with Destiny had been booked for thirty-eight weeks and I didn't go into early labour. She was born at thirty-eight weeks because she was healthy and was growing bigger in my tummy so the doctors decided to take her out early. She weighed nearly four kilograms at birth. The doctors said that if we waited one more week, she would weigh five or even six kilograms, which would have been difficult for me to carry. Dorcas was born at thirty-seven weeks weighing just two and a half kilos.

At twenty weeks I was consumed with fear and anxiety. I feared that I might lose my baby again at twenty-one weeks but I was happy when I reached twenty-four weeks and my baby was doing well in the womb. The stress and anxiety caused me to have a severe dizzy episode at twenty-five weeks but I didn't end up going to the hospital for treatment. Instead, I stayed home and I recovered well a few hours later.

The doctors had told me to prepare for the worst during and after birth. They said that even though Dorcas's CPAM condition had remained the same, there was a possibility that she might not be able to breathe on her own and that they might need to perform surgery straight away. They said that if Dorcas cried loudly after she was born, that would indicate that she might not need to have surgery immediately, though she might still need to have surgery before she turned six months or one year old. They said that if she came out and did not cry, she would be rushed into surgery before my own wound was stitched.

On the morning that Dorcas was born, I had over ten specialist medical staff in my surgery room, including the baby's surgeons and their helpers, my surgeons and their helpers, the paediatricians, midwives, intensive care unit staff and theatre nurses ready to take my baby to surgery. But God did it for me and Dorcas came out screaming very loudly and she couldn't stop screaming. Everyone clapped and laughed and said that she had very strong lungs. Even though she had a hundred percent oxygen level from birth, she was still taken to intensive care to be monitored for six hours to make sure that she was okay, and sure enough she was. When she was six months old, she had a check-up at the WCH and the specialist told me that she did not need to have surgery because she was 'very healthy'. The doctor said that whatever I was doing with her, I should keep doing it because it was working. I still take her to the hospital for X-rays and check-ups once a year to monitor the CPAM in her lung but so far, so good.

I was weak after surgery and kept going in and out of consciousness because I had lost too much blood and my haemoglobin had gone down to ninety-five percent. I was kept in the recovery room next to the surgery room for more than two hours. I couldn't feel my legs and I was too weak to open my eyes, which was not a good sign.

Many times I could hear the doctors calling my name and asking me to squeeze their hands and open my eyes but I couldn't respond or open my eyes for more than two hours. After some time, I finally opened my eyes and I was able to respond to the doctors but I was still not able to sit up. Four hours later, I was taken to a ward where I was reunited with my baby. The first time I tried to sit up five hours after surgery, I felt dizzy and I fell back on the bed. I took a sip of water, felt sick and I vomited non-stop for more than three minutes. The doctors were called to my room and they gave me medication to stop the vomiting after they examined me, and I recovered well and quickly.

Two days later, I was discharged from the ward and out of the hospital because there were other women waiting for beds. There were not enough beds at the WCH at the time and they were discharging women very early as a result. Clearly, I was not well enough to leave the hospital but they discharged me anyway. Luckily, a parliamentary politician who had come to visit me was with me in the room at the time and she launched a complaint to the hospital boss on my behalf. The hospital boss later issued an apology to me through the politician. She claimed that she didn't know such practices were happening in the hospital and that she was going to make sure it didn't happen again. The hospital boss told the politician to ask me to put my complaint in writing and said they would compensate me if my early discharge resulted in complicated medical issues or if it had jeopardised my recovery, but I was well and there was no need for that.

This was the second time the hospital boss had to issue an apology to me for bad treatment. After my first daughter was born, the midwives looking after me made racist and discriminatory remarks about me, my disability and South Sudanese women in general, stating that South Sudanese women were having a lot of children and were receiving a lot of money from Centrelink because of their big families and yet they had no English skills and were unemployed. The other midwife said that I was not going to be able to look after my daughter because of my disability and that the burden of looking after my daughter was going to fall back onto the government. She also said that the only reason why I had my baby was to get money from Centrelink! She said that refugee women with disabilities like me should not be allowed to have children as they themselves are a waste of space. For two days, I didn't eat at the hospital and I had to order food from outside. Those two midwives had refused to allow the hospital food company to bring food to my room by advising them that I had been discharged while I was still there. Some of my food in the fridge that I had ordered from outside the hospital had also gone missing. I had to involve the hospital social worker, who also launched a complaint to the boss on my behalf. The hospital boss came to my ward to apologise to me in person and she offered me a job as a cultural consultant and a disability advocate at the WCH but I couldn't take the job because the timing was not right. They did, however, later employ another South Sudanese woman as the hospital's cultural consultant.

When I was thirty weeks pregnant with Dorcas, I was diagnosed with gestational diabetes. The doctors said that one in four women suffer from gestational diabetes after losing a pregnancy and that it was nothing for me to worry about because my blood sugar level would go back to normal as soon as the baby was born, but that I still needed to continue eating healthy food and also exercise when I could. They said that because there was no history of diabetes or high blood pressure in my family, I would be healthy after my baby was born but only if I ate healthy food and exercised often; if I fell into unhealthy eating habits, there was a fifty percent chance of me developing type 2 diabetes, they said. My third daughter was born in May 2016. A day after she was born, my blood sugar level went back to normal and her blood sugar level was also normal.

Seventeen

OVERCOMING THE STIGMA
OF BEING A SINGLE MOTHER
WITH A DISABILITY

Being a parent is hard enough, let alone being a single mother with a disability from a refugee background with no family support network. I consider some parents lucky because they have parents, grandparents, aunties and uncles who are able to help with caring for their children so they can have time out or time to themselves. Other parents with no family support network have their husbands there to support them, but I am all alone and I have to juggle everything by myself, including studies, work and parenting as well as dealing with the late effects of polio — fatigue, headaches, body pain, loss of muscle functioning, bone and joint pain and general body exhaustion.

I had to cancel my elbow surgery in March 2020 due to the coronavirus pandemic lockdown, because I didn't have anybody to look after my children while I would be in the hospital. My sister and my friends were self-isolating and I could not solely rely on my support workers to look after my children full time as they come and go. If I had a permanent carer who lived with me fulltime, I would have been able to have the surgery. When my children are sick and I am also sick, I have to stay awake all night and all day the following day and the days after to look after my children until they are feeling better and then I can focus on getting well myself. I can't take pain medication when my children are sick because I risk becoming drowsy and dozing off to sleep. I have to stay awake and in pain for my children and then I can take my pain medication when my children are better.

One day in October 2013 when Jimmy and I had just started talking, I woke up at 4am with severe dizziness and I had to go to the hospital in an ambulance with my daughter. She was nearly three years old and she had to finish her night's sleep on my hospital bed that morning. We were discharged at 9am and my sister drove us home. My sister was working night shift at the same hospital that night (she is a nurse). I specifically asked to be taken to that hospital so that my sister could take my daughter home if I was to stay at the hospital for longer. I rang Jimmy that morning several times to help me but he didn't answer and he didn't ring me back for the whole week. I suffer from low blood pressure and low iron which has resulted in the on and off dizziness episodes.

In February 2019, Dorcas had a high temperature and we had to go to the hospital in the middle of the night but this time I couldn't drag Destiny out of bed to go to the hospital with us. Instead, I rang Jimmy and this time he answered and he came to look after Destiny in the house. I also rang my sister and we went to the hospital together. She wasn't working that night. It was midnight when we got there and we were discharged at 2:30am when her temperature had gone down.

I love my children to bits but it would also be nice to have time to myself once in a while to recharge and to regain the energy to be able to keep up with them. My children are very active. Right now, I have no backup energy left in me and I'm sure that when my girls are older and I finally am able to have time to myself, I might spend a long period of time recovering from overusing my polio muscles for many years. I had two nights without my children in September 2019, when I went to Port Elliot. Two of my friends helped care for my children while I was away. I went back to the same place Jimmy and I stayed in 2015 to reconnect with those emotions, which has helped me to let go of him. It would be nice to have more of those nights away. But at least I have my children in my life. I don't know what life would be like for me without my children in it. I am also happy because I know that God is in control and that he is always refilling my cup by recharging my energy every time I have a little sleep.

I am doing my very best to raise my children to be good citizens and to also be God-fearing women, for the Bible says that, 'The fear of God is the beginning of Wisdom' (Proverbs 9:10). I am also doing my very best to educate my children so that they can obtain educational qualifications. It would be my absolute pleasure to see my children graduate from university, get their first jobs, get married and have children. I would love for them to live with me until they are married and then they can move out but I can only guide them and leave the rest to God. When they are older, they can make their own decisions and I will support them in whatever they want to do.

The biggest difficulty of being a single mother is that I hardly get time to myself to do adult things, like go out to dinner with friends or go somewhere for a night or a weekend like I did in September 2019 because I don't have that kind of support of having someone to look after my children. I always have to wait until my friends are available and are able to help me. I can't just get up and go somewhere for the weekend whenever I like. It is also hard for me to go out to the movies, Bible study, and dinner with my single-mother friends without our children as they also don't have anyone to help them.

Some people who are in my situation say that they help each other by looking after each other's children in order to have time out but, to be honest, I don't have the energy to look after other people's children as well as looking after my own due to the fatigue and body exhaustion I have at the end of every day. And that would also disrupt my children's sleep time. I have organised myself in such a way that by 8pm, my children have finished dinner and are sleeping so that I can rest before I go to bed between 9:30pm and 11pm. My children eat dinner between 5:30pm and 6:30pm at the latest so they can do homework, have a play and then read a book before they go to bed. My children and I never sleep during the day, even on weekends, public holidays or during school holidays, so that we can go to sleep early, wake up and be ready for the next day by 8am for school or 9am on weekends, public holidays or during school holidays to do housework, attend sports, go shopping or simply go to the park for a play. Some people I know sleep during the day and they start cooking dinner at 7pm and their children will go to bed between 10pm and 12midnight, even on school days. That arrangement works for them and their children but I couldn't live like that. Sleep is very important to me and to my growing little children, that's why I let my children sleep for at least ten hours every night.

Part of my self-organisation is also to go without other things in my life to be able to send my daughters to child care and after-school care four days a week so that I can be able to write my books, attend appointments, go out to lunch with friends, do other things and rest before I pick them up. My children going to child care and after-school care is not good for the pocket but it's good because it enables me to do other things without interruption. If I didn't organise myself in this way, I would not have been able to study, complete my Master's degree and write my books. Recently, I have started to receive support with transporting my children from school and with afterhours childcare funded by the National Disability Insurance Scheme, which is a huge relief, but at the moment I am not able to go out to meet anyone for dinner because of the physical isolation and social distancing restrictions put in place to stop the spread of coronavirus. Once the social distancing restriction has been lifted, I will finally be able to go out to dinner and perhaps meet someone.

Because African girls are considered to be a source of income in many African cultures, including South Sudanese culture, they are expected to get married and bring wealth to their families in the form of a dowry. Having a disability means not much chance of marriage and therefore no wealth, so girls and women with disabilities are disowned by some parents. My qualifications do not earn me respect in my community; marriage is what earns me respect. Because I am not married and because I am a single mother with a disability, I have no respect from most people in my community. Many people think that because I am a single mother and because I have had children from two different men, that I must be rich because the fathers of my daughters must be paying me child support. Others have even said that I never wanted to be with a man and that's the reason why I kicked the biological fathers of my daughters out! There are many single mothers in my community with different circumstances but people have summed them up in three words, that 'they love money', that's why they are single because, apparently, Centrelink pays a lot of money to single parents on top of the child support they must receive from the fathers of their children. Always when a relationship fails, the first thing people in my community talk about is money.

Nobody believes that I don't receive child support.

When people come to my house and see how well I have kept my house and how my children and I live, they automatically think that I am either receiving big money from the government, including child support, or that I have a man living with me who is giving me money. People think that single mothers are not able to provide for their children without child support from the fathers. People also say that there is no way a single mother with a disability without a family support network like me could manage to keep it all together. Someone recently asked me on Facebook how come I was single and still beautiful and happy. My response to him was that I did not need to be married and I did not need a man to be happy. My happiness is from God and it's also from within me.

People think that if you are a single mother, you should be unhappy and miserable, and your children should look different or your children must be criminals. Every time there is a break-in or a car has been stolen somewhere, people will automatically conclude that the children of single mothers have committed the crime. One night I was sitting at a dining table in a house with my daughter where we attended Bible study and afterwards people were talking about disrespectful children, including children of single parents. The lady who hosted the Bible study said that, 'it is official that children of single parents are untrained and are criminals'. I got up and left and I never went back to that house again. I also stopped going to that Church because it didn't feel right for me to pray in the same Church with people I considered hypocrites. They were supposed to support everyone in their Church, including single parents, not to judge them.

I am aware that there are some single mothers in my community who are struggling emotionally, financially and with everything else, and that could be because they don't know how to manage the little money they have, they have mental health issues, they feel lonely or maybe because they are not content with what they have, and because of that they may need help. But people should stop making assumptions that every single mother is the same. I am also aware that some single mothers in my community are having multiple sexual relationships with different men and they even bring those men into their house and introduce them to their children as uncles but then the uncles will sleep in mummy's room. Three or four months later, that relationship is finished and they are off to another relationship. They will bring another 'uncle' to the house again. Some of them even end up having more children with the so-called uncles, which can be very confusing and damaging not only to their children but also to the women themselves. But I want to clarify that not every single mother is like that. Some single mothers like me have far better things to do with our time and with our lives.

Some single parents I know have tried to copy my lifestyle in order to have everything together and to live a 'happy' life, like my children and I do, but they ended up creating more problems for themselves. They think that I must have a lot of money because I am happy, so they tried to make and find big money the wrong way and they instead end up creating more problems for themselves because they are not content with what they have. In reality, these people who have tried to copy my lifestyle have more money than I do. I sat down with two of them on separate occasions to talk about money and we discovered that they were receiving up to $1,500 a fortnight more than me but their lives and that of their children were still crumbling because they didn't know how to budget well. They felt ashamed after they found out that I am able to keep everything together with the little money I have and there they were, complaining about every little thing when they should actually be helping people like me. My message to everyone reading this book is to never copy other people's lifestyle, never compare yourself with others and never compete with others but learn to be content with what you have and try to find happiness from within you. Do not base your happiness on a man, on anyone or on material things but put your trust in God and try to be happy with what you have rather than worrying about what you don't have. The things of this world will pass but God's love and happiness is forever. If you have a man in your life who loves you and treats you well, be grateful and please stop comparing him to other men or other people's husbands. We are all different and unique in our own way so let us celebrate our uniqueness without comparing ourselves to others. Don't get me wrong, there is nothing wrong in having money. We all need money to pay our rent, mortgages and bills and buy food, but the love for money is bad and it might take us to an early grave.

Some men in my community think that because a woman is a single mother, she must be desperate for sex and they assume that she must be allowing men, including married men, to sleep with her to satisfy those men's sexual needs. Like I mentioned earlier, there are some single mothers in my community who bring 'uncles' to their houses to sleep with and once a man from my community succeeds in sleeping with them, those men will go out into the community and tell other men to also try their luck and, in most cases, the other men will also succeed in sleeping with them and the cycle will continue. This has made some men in my community think that all single mothers are the same and that they now have the right to judge all single mothers, including me, based on other single mothers' behaviours, not knowing that some single mothers like myself have far more better things to do with my life and time than to simply lay down and sleep around with them. I want my children to remember me as a good role model to them and to others when I am gone. To be a role model, I have to sacrifice a lot and live by example. I hope my children will be proud of me and of the things I have done for them.

Eighteen

BUDGETING AND MANAGING A SINGLE INCOME AS A SINGLE MOTHER

Before and when I was pregnant with my first child, Destiny, I was working and not receiving the Disability Support Pension from Centrelink. My DSP was cancelled in 2008 two weeks after I started working with Families SA. My gross income was twice that of the DSP but I was receiving a mobility allowance of $60 a fortnight from Centrelink to enable me to commute to and from work. My DSP was reinstated in September 2010 after I stopped working. I was heavily pregnant, at seven months, with Destiny. Ten months after Destiny was born, I went back to work three days a week in 2011 and I also returned to study my Master's degree. My DSP was cancelled after I returned to work but I was receiving family payments this time and mobility allowance. In July 2013, I stopped working and went back to study full time because the University of South Australia was not going to offer the Master's degree in Mediation and Conflict Resolution past 2014, so all the students that were already enrolled in the course had to finish the degree by November 2014. My DSP was reinstated and has not been cancelled since.

In March 2015, after I completed my studies, I went back to work on a contract basis for two days a week. I was pregnant with Hannah and then with Dorcas and was not able to work more than two days a week. I worked with the Young Women's Christian Association in Adelaide as a project coordinator for the Crossing the Bridge Project, which was meant to support African women with disabilities in South Australia. I was the founder of the project. I was receiving part of the DSP and my salary plus family payments as well as mobility allowance. In late 2015, my mobility allowance was cancelled because I stopped travelling to work. I did work from home a little bit before I stopped. This time I was heavily pregnant with Dorcas.

In 2012, after I completed writing the project, I spoke with the then Dignity Party SA leader, the Honourable Kelly Vincent, to seek her support and she was able to link me with the Young Women's Christian Association. The YWCA CEO and I applied for funding together and we were lucky to secure two and a half years of federal funding. I marketed and promoted the project and, within six months, it was up and running. I set up group activities, including sewing classes, information sessions and networking, to African women with disabilities in South Australia. I was also able to identify stakeholders for the project and we held quarterly stakeholder meetings to monitor and evaluate the progress of my project. I submitted monthly reports to the YWCA and quarterly progress reports to the government.

In August 2015, during our stakeholder meeting, I requested that we employ another staff member from the African community to help me with managing the group activities, and the stakeholders agreed. Since I started working on the project, I had received very limited support from the YWCA and I was becoming overwhelmed with the amount of work I was doing single-handedly. I also became worried in October that year that I might lose my pregnancy again if I continued working overtime the way I did. I worked seven days a week with some work done from home after hours, on the days I was not supposed to be working and on weekends, but I was paid a salary for only two days a week. I also continued working from home without pay months after I had taken unpaid maternity leave. I also used my own car for work purposes but I wasn't reimbursed for mileage. Weeks earlier, before I went on unpaid maternity leave, two of the stakeholder members had advised me to take time off work and look after myself and my pregnancy. I did take time off work and I left the newly employed Ethiopian woman to manage the project but I was still working from home on the phone to support her without pay. I couldn't go back to work immediately after Dorcas was born because of her lung condition (described in Chapter 16). I worried about taking her to child care before she was eight months old because if she caught a cold, it would complicate her breathing. I was waiting for the doctors' verdict at six months old to see if she would have surgery and if it was safe to take her to childcare or not. The project funding ran out in the meantime and the YWCA CEO contacted me to write a support letter to apply for more funding, which I did and this time the government gave the YWCA three years funding for the project.

In January 2017, I organised to meet with the YWCA CEO and the YWCA community programs manager to present my case and to see if I could work from home for a few weeks to start with and then I would gradually go back to work in the office. The CEO refused to let me work from home, stating that there was no guarantee I would not be using that paid time to look after my 'sick' baby. She also told me that they had shifted the focus of my project from supporting African women with disabilities to supporting older African women (Ethiopian women) in South Australia and that it was no longer a problem for them if I didn't return to work.

In July 2018, I contacted the woman managing the project to inform her that I was ready to return to work one day a week but she told me that she didn't need my help anymore. She was working three days a week but she couldn't give one day a week to me. I was the one who convinced the YWCA to employ her but she couldn't return the favour. Without me, she would not have received that job but she turned her back on me after she was settled in the job! She has taught me a lesson and I will certainly be careful in the future if I have the opportunity to employ staff or if I find myself again in a position where I am able to recommend people for employment. I do, however, think that everything happens for a reason. Even though I didn't receive any recognition from the YWCA for my hard work, I did at least receive an award from the African community as an acknowledgement of my work with African women with disabilities, which I do appreciate and it makes me feel like I matter. It has boosted my confidence and positivity towards life and my community.

I did mention in my first book that I would be looking forward to returning to work once my youngest daughter started school but I am now ready to return to work before she starts school. I have renewed my police clearance, passport and memberships, including my mediation membership with the Australian Mediation Association. I thought that I could return to work in May 2020 to save some money for my children's school fees but this has been put on hold because of the coronavirus pandemic. In the meantime, I enrolled to do some online mediation top-up courses in June and in October 2020 and I have also started to apply for jobs. My national mediation accreditation expired two years ago and, also because I have not been practising as a mediator in the last two years, I had to do the online top-up/refresher courses and be reassessed to be nationally accredited as a mediator again.

Esther received a community award for her work in the Adelaide community with African women with disabilities

Whether I am working and earning salary or just receiving DSP, I have always managed my finances well to be able to pay rent, bills, school and childcare fees and also buy food. My daughters went to a private childcare centre because that was the closest and are also going to a private Christian school. I pay subsidised school and childcare fees. My rent is paid through Centrelink's Centrepay service and I have organised to pay my bills fortnightly. By the time the invoices arrive, I have already paid most of the bill and then I will just pay what is left. Sometimes I have already paid the amount on the next bill and they just send me a letter to inform me that the bill has been paid. When my daughters were two months old, I opened bank accounts for them and I pay $50 each into their accounts every fortnight. I make sure I don't touch their accounts unless I have to. For example, when we were living in the expensive private house near the airport and I didn't have money in my account for bills after paying the rent, I withdrew money from my children's accounts to pay for bills. I would also withdraw money from their accounts if it is time to pay school fees and if I don't have any money in my own account. After we moved out of the private rental back to the public housing and then to the community housing, I was able to start saving again but only for a very short period of time.

I always buy vegetables and meat, including onions and okra, fish, chicken, dry beans, rice, semolina, cooking oil, long-life milk and meat as well as washing detergent and cleaning stuff in bulk and I cook at home from scratch. Once I stock my freezer and pantry with food, I do not shop for non-perishable groceries for two to three months, which has enabled me to save some money. I don't buy pre-packaged food, frozen vegetables, canned food or readily cooked food because they are small portions and expensive. Canned and frozen food are also not fresh like the vegetables you buy from a fruit and vegetable shop. The meat I buy from the butcher is bigger and fresher than pre-packaged meat from the supermarket. I eat out or eat takeaway only a few times a year to help me save money. I have recently started growing my own vegetables (spinach, spring onions, tomatoes and more) in my backyard to also help me save money. I basically buy everything in bulk and spend $400 or more on two to three months of non-perishable groceries and freeze the ones that needs freezing. I will buy perishable things like bread, fruit, green vegetables and other things only once a week and when I need to. I know places where I can buy fresh food for less. I think that growing up in the refugee camps has enabled me to appreciate life and to manage the little money that I have very well. I know that a lot of people are complaining that the DSP is very low and yes, it is, but if you budget well and if the whole DSP is not going towards expensive rent, you will be able to save money from the DSP. I have not been able to travel since

I came to Australia fifteen years ago because of having to pay childcare and school fees and my car loan repayments, but a time will come when I will be able to travel and go on holidays when my children are older.

In August 2018, I had a car accident and my insurance company gave me some money, which I paid as a deposit on my new car. I took a $32,000 car loan on finance from Toyota and Toyota was able to give me a low repayment rate per month based on my DSP and family payments. It will take me seven years to pay back the loan but I am managing. In 2019 especially, I struggled with registering and insuring my car because the little money that I usually save for this is now going into repaying my car loan, but I am glad that I am still able to sleep at night regardless of my financial hardships. I am also able to wake up every morning feeling fresh and manage to keep a big smile on my face and still keep everything together. Even in the midst of my financial hardship, I am still able to put food on the table. Not a single day has passed that my children and I have gone without food.

Esther picking up her new car from CMI Toyota
in Adelaide in 2018

In March 2019, I self-published my first book, *Beyond Calamity*, with Fontaine Publishing Group. Self-publishing my first book and taking a car loan has set me back big time financially. I did have some money saved in my account in 2018 but I used that money to finalise the publication of my first book. I now find that some fortnights, my account balance is negative because I don't have enough money to pay for everything. In February 2020, I wanted to have more copies of my first book printed but I couldn't because I didn't have the money. Since my first book was published, I have been invited to speak at community and Church events and schools to share my story and to promote my book, where I have been able to sell a few books here and there, and I have been able to use the money from book sales on fuel and on accessible cabs to get to and from the hospital. Between August 2018 and February 2020, I spent more than $500 on transport to and from the hospital. Even with the fifty percent taxi vouchers that I have, I still spend a lot of money on access cabs for hospital appointments, when I use the wheelchair. Now that I have had my car modified (funded by the NDIS) and I am able to take my folding scooter everywhere with me in the boot of my car, I will hopefully not spend a lot of money on access cabs from now on.

Esther in a wheelchair at Victoria Square in Adelaide

Sometimes I get invited to speak at community events and I will end up not selling a single book, like in November 2019, when a woman who worked for a Church organisation came to me to ask for ideas and advice to enable her to host a successful event and I helped her. Two days later, she sent me an invitation to be the keynote speaker in one of her workshops and I agreed. She even used my family picture and profile to advertise the workshop but she didn't allow me to speak and I didn't sell any books. She condensed a whole-day workshop into two and a half hours. A lady with vison impairment was to open the event with a five-minute song and then I would speak for ten to fifteen minutes after the formal introductions. After my speech we would break into small group discussions which would be followed by lunch break and networking and then we would all come back into a large group discussion after lunch. I was to sell my books after the workshop formalities were finished but she allowed the lady to sing five songs for more than thirty minutes and she also included other speakers in the program which I was not aware of. People got bored and others left while the singing was still going. She panicked and she opened the floor for introductions. I started introducing myself first but she took the microphone off me less than two minutes into my introduction. I felt embarrassed because I had not even finished introducing myself but I put myself together and stayed. I could have left but I didn't. She tried to rush the whole program but half the people left before lunch break and almost everyone left after lunch. I didn't even get to talk about my book and I also left. I cancelled other important appointments to be at that event but I didn't even get to speak, nor did I sell any books. There were about fifty people at the workshop and I was confident that I would be able to sell at least five books or more that day but I sold nothing. I have also been invited to community events and told to bring a few books with me, which I do, but the organisers leave it until the end of the event to introduce me. By that time, most people have already left. I have also had to leave some events before the organisers introduced me because the event formalities took too long and it was time for my babysitter to go home.

Esther speaking at an International
Women's Day dinner in Adelaide in 2017

Some people, including some community leaders in the South Sudanese community, have taken books from me but have not been able to pay for the books. When I'm at events, someone will come and talk to me at my table where my books are displayed and others would take advantage of that moment to take books from the table and then walk away without paying. By the time I finished talking to the other person, two or three books have gone missing and I don't know who has taken them. The people do not come back to pay for the books, they just disappear. Others will take the books and pretend to be transferring money into my account because they don't have cash when I am talking or signing a book for someone else. By the time I have finished, the person who was making the transfer is gone. I go to check my account and there is no money transferred. When I confront them later, others would say that they thought I gave the book to them as a gift. Others would say that they will return the book, stating that they cannot pay $30 for such a small book, but when I tell them to return the book, they will not. Some bookshops in Adelaide are selling my books for more than $40. The online price is more than $30, including postage, but I bring my books to the people and sell them for $30 and they still say that my book is expensive. This is how bad things are in my community. South Sudanese people do not support each other because they are either divided or they are jealous of other people's achievements, and they will either pull them down or try to jeopardise their business. Some people in my community think that for someone to publish a book that person must be rich and they think that taking a book or two for free will not result in losses. Others still do not understand that I have had to spend big money to publish and print the book and that I need to recover this money by selling the books and not give them away for free.

There are people I know in my community who have tried to open small businesses here in South Australia but their businesses have collapsed within a few months because people in my community go to their shops to take things without paying for them. African people will never go to shops run by non-African people to take things for free but when it comes to African shops or businesses, all of a sudden, they don't have money and will take things for free. I have also given away more than fifty books for publicity. I hope I don't encounter the same problems with my second book.

Even though I do not belong to the rich or middle class of Australians, I have chosen to enrol my children into a private childcare centre and now into a private school but I have been able to pay subsidised school fees and childcare fees. I have always paid my daughter's school fees in full. As soon as I have paid one year's school fees, I start putting money aside for the next year and I make sure that I don't touch that money. I pay the childcare fees fortnightly because, even with childcare subsidy, childcare is more expensive than the subsidised school fees. I can take my child out of childcare at any time if I want to so there is no need to pay the childcare fees in full even if I could afford to.

I have not been able to put enough money aside for school fees since I started repaying my car loan from late 2018 but Jimmy has been able to help me with a little money in 2019 and in January 2020 towards my daughter's school fees and piano lessons. Jimmy also paid for my daughter's soccer fees for one term in 2018 and for two terms in 2019. My daughter played soccer with Grasshopper Soccer in Adelaide from late 2016 until the end of term two in 2019. She is not playing soccer now because she injured her heel at school gymnastics in 2017 and she has been getting on and off pain in her heel since. I have been asking Jimmy since January 2017 to pay for our daughter's childcare fees but he has refused. He has instead started giving me $200 a month from November 2019 towards my car loan repayments and he has also given me some money towards my daughter's school fees. It is very little money but it's better than nothing. Jimmy has recently told me that the reason why he refused to pay for our daughter's childcare fees is because I am staying at home and doing nothing. He said that it is my responsibility as her mother to care for our daughter at home since I am not working but because I chose to take our daughter to child care, I should pay that fees myself. He said that he would only pay childcare fees if I was working. I find it more convenient to pay the school fees in full and then forget about it until the next year. Paying in full also entitles me to a five percent discount of $100, which goes back into my pocket to help pay for other things. There is no discount if I pay the fees fortnightly or quarterly.

Even though Jimmy has somehow come around and is now willing to give me some money when he feels like it, I don't want to rock the boat by asking him for child support. I was hoping that Jimmy and I could make a private arrangement for him to pay for our children's child care, school fees, extracurricular activities and sports without involving the courts but this is still not working. If Jimmy gave me money for school fees or to buy things for our children like he did in January 2020, he would stop giving me the $200 for my car loan repayments for three months and then he would start again. Also if Jimmy and I had a disagreement about something, he would stop giving me money all together. He is using his money as a weapon and as a tool to punish me. A few friends of mine have asked me to take him to court and force him to pay child support and also have him put in jail because of the way he has treated me and my children but I refused. They said that the child support money would continue coming into my account regardless of whether he had spent some money on the girls or not but I have refused. Unfortunately, I have lost some of those friends as a result. These were the same friends that stood by my side in 2016 after Jimmy left. They said that I was protecting him and they didn't like it so we parted ways. According to them, Jimmy does not deserve this much protection, respect, loyalty, devotion and love from me after the emotional torture he and his relatives put me through. I am receiving exempt family payments from Centrelink.

Esther sitting in her car, about to drive to a
traditional wedding ceremony in 2019

Like the school fees, I pay my car registration and insurance once a year and then I also forget about it. Before my car loan, I used to take my car to be serviced when the service was due and I used to go to the shops to buy clothes and other things without even thinking or checking my bank account to check if I had money. Now, I have to check my account and think about whether to take my car for a service or whether to go clothes and shoes shopping or not. Even if I have a little bit of money left in my account after paying rent, the money will only be for basic things like food and bills. If I use that money to service my car or to buy clothes and shoes, I will not be able to pay my next bills in time. Things are a little bit tight for me now financially but things will get better soon. Going back to work would ease the financial pressure a little bit but I can't go back to work until the coronavirus lockdown has been lifted. Even then, I still don't know what going back to work post-pandemic is going to look like for me.

In late 2016, after I had used all my savings on rent and didn't have money left over to buy food, clothes or shoes, I started to go to Anglicare to collect food. I was embarrassed to go and ask for food but I had no choice if I was going to be able to put dinner on the table. After eleven years in Australia, I thought that I was settled and I was actually doing better than most people, considering my situation. Going to ask for food again from charity organisations like Anglicare or the Salvation Army was the last thing on my mind. The first time I went to Anglicare and was provided with food and clothes vouchers, I was afraid to walk out to my car with the food because I was worried that I would meet someone I knew and that person might ask me what I was doing collecting food from Anglicare. A volunteer from Anglicare helped me carry my food to the car but I couldn't stop looking from side to side to see who was there watching. I was also worried that if people saw me, they would tell Jimmy that I was collecting food from Anglicare because I was not able to provide food for myself and my children and that might make him want to apply for full custody of our children. The thought of losing my children to him because I was not able to provide food for them without the support of Anglicare and some friends at the time scared me to death. I could not ask for support from my community because I didn't want to be a laughing stock, I didn't want to become a hot topic of gossip and I also didn't want people telling Jimmy that I was begging for food from the community. On the other hand, I didn't want to beg Jimmy for money because I didn't want to lose my children to him so I pretended like everything was okay and that I was on top of everything. Clearly, despite my bright face and big smile, I was sad, angry, embarrassed and I felt alone and lost but I came out of that situation to the other side even stronger than I was before.

The Anglicare staff member who interviewed me saw that I was nervous and uncomfortable but she told me that it was okay. She said that going to Anglicare to collect food was nothing to be embarrassed about and that it was not the end of the world. She said that they saw middle-class people walk through their doors after a relationship breakdown and the partner who had become homeless would come to them for food and accommodation. I was allowed to visit them four times a year to collect food and clothes vouchers to enable me to collect food from their food store and clothes from their op shop. The food vouchers were for twenty-five food items per visit — twenty-two non-perishable and three perishable food items. I didn't need to visit Anglicare four times a year because the twenty-two non-perishable food items I collected lasted me three months. I went to Anglicare once in late 2016, twice in 2017 and once in early 2018.

I didn't want to be reminded of my first few years in Australia when I relied solely on the Australian Refugee Association and the Salvation Army for food but there I was, eleven years later, still collecting food and clothes for my children from charity organisations when I should have been the one helping those in need. History was repeating itself except that this time things were different. I wasn't a refugee anymore, I was an Australian citizen and I also had children. It was not only me to think about but I also had to think about my children. Between

December 2016 and December 2019, Anglicare and some of my friends, my sister, my Church and Dignity Party SA provided me with formula and nappies, clothes and shoes for my children, especially on their birthdays. My advice to anyone reading this book is that no matter how hard things get and no matter how dark the world around you gets, never give up because there is always light at the end of the tunnel.

Nineteen

MY WRITING JOURNEY IN ENGLISH AS A SECOND LANGUAGE

Esther signing her book Beyond Calamity during her book launch in June 2019

To me, writing didn't come automatically but I have had to work really hard to make sure that what I have written down sounds right and it makes sense. Writing a book in English as a second language meant that I had to read out loud in a quiet place so many times to connect what I was reading to what I was hearing, from my mouth to my ears. Sometimes, I have had to rewrite a sentence or a paragraph so many times for it to sound better. When I am sitting in my small writing room, ideas and words come as I write but then I realise that because I am writing about my life journey, where there are a lot of raw emotions involved, I feel like I have been taken back and I am reliving the situation all over again. I have had to debrief with a few friends with my second book, especially in the area of relationships, but without talking in detail about what I have written and without letting my friends read the manuscript first. I used to think in another language and then translate into English when writing or speaking but I am glad that I am now able to think and write in English. Even then, I still find that I am taking twice as long to write a book compared to other people who write in English as their first language.

Publishing my first book has motivated me to write this, my second book. The feedback I have received from people about my first book so far has been overwhelming and encouraging. People said that my first book was inspiring and powerful not only for women but also for men and for children over ten years of age. People said that *Beyond Calamity* was well written and that it was written from the heart. Others said that, 'if you read *Beyond Calamity*, your life will never be the same again', that the way you view and approach life will change for the better. Someone recently told me that my book had changed the way he related to his wife and how he treated her. Like any other couple, this couple had their own fair share of ups and downs but after reading my first book, he reports that they are now a happy couple. Who would have thought that my humble story in my first book could have such a big impact in people's lives, by saving marriages and restoring relationships!

Some people have come to me in person to my house or out in the community to thank me for writing and also inspiring them through my first book. Other people have reached out to me via email, Facebook, messenger and phone calls. People have said that the first thing that strikes you when you see *Beyond Calamity* is the beautiful, eye-catching book cover. I gave my publisher a detailed description of what I wanted the cover to look like and they came up with this beautiful book cover. I probably provided my publisher with too much and confusing information but they were able to narrow it down to the image you see on the cover. People also said that the book title and subtitle were unique and attention-grabbing. A manager at Dymocks bookshop in Adelaide said that he had never in his book-selling business come across a book that looked like mine with a title like *Beyond Calamity*. Wow, I am so honoured and very thankful to Vivid Publishing, part of Fontaine Publishing Group, in Fremantle, Western Australia, for editing, designing and publishing my beautiful book and for getting my book out to the public. Without Fontaine, I would not have been able to achieve all this in the world of writing. I hope my second book will receive the same or an even better response.

People want to know how long it took me to write a book that is such a good read. Here is the answer. *Beyond Calamity* is the story of my life journey, contracting polio in South Sudan as a four-year-old girl and surviving that, growing up in three different refugee camps in Uganda, growing up and overcoming challenges as a girl and as a woman with a disability in the South Sudanese community, migrating to Australia as a refugee in 2005 and overcoming challenges on a daily basis as a woman and as a single mother with a disability from a refugee background. I started writing it in 2010. It was hard to write at the beginning because I was overcome with emotions. Every time I wrote a sentence or a paragraph, I would cry and have sleepless nights but when I started to think about what my story would do to others and how my story might encourage others, writing the book became easier. After I had written five chapters, I started looking for a publisher. I googled and the first name that came up from my google search was Fontaine Publishing Group. I contacted them with a brief summary of my story. The following day, I received an email from Fontaine, stating that they were interested in editing and publishing my book. They proposed their assisted self-publishing pathway and I agreed with that option.

The difficulty with the self-publishing option is that I had to have money ready for my book to be edited, designed and published. I also had to do everything by myself, including marketing, promoting my book, organising my book launch and basically selling my book by myself. But I think that I have done a really good job with marketing and promoting my book by attending radio and newsletter interviews, meetings and events, and via Facebook, email and phone.

The first invoice came and I organised the payment and then I sent my manuscript to Fontaine. By this time, I had already written over ten chapters. The editor there at the time sent my manuscript back, asking me to rewrite it then send it back to her. She said that my manuscript was more academic than a novel. A few months later, I finished rewriting and sent it back but the editor sent my manuscript back to me for a second pass.

She told me that if I was that serious about writing, maybe I should first join a book writing club to learn the craft. Once I had done that, I should revisit my manuscript from scratch, referencing other African female authors, and then send it back to her. Following this advice, I didn't touch or look at my manuscript again until early 2017. During that period of silence, I had this burning feeling, urge and pushing desire inside of me telling me to write that novel and publish it. As soon as I started rewriting my manuscript from scratch in early 2017, the burning feeling inside of me stopped. It was then that I realised I was ready to publish my first book.

In April 2018, I contacted Fontaine again to say that I had rewritten my manuscript from scratch and believed it was ready for editing and publishing. They responded straight away and I sent them the rewritten manuscript. This time another editor worked on my manuscript. This is what she said after reading it:

'Esther, I feel privileged and honoured to be the one editing your manuscript.'

'Your manuscript is well written, you used good language and plain English to write your manuscript and it reads really well.'

'Your story has made me think of the privileges we have here in Australia which in most cases, we take for granted.'

'Esther, I can hear your voice in every sentence and every paragraph and it is humbling.'

'I hope that our politicians will get to read your book and it will hopefully help them to make informed decisions in relation to refugees and asylum seeker issues in Australia.'

The first editor had told me to rewrite my book in the third person voice so that my story wouldn't identify me in my community as the message in my manuscript was a very sensitive one. She also thought that writing in the third person would give me a higher chance of my book selling well. In other words, she said that fiction books sell better than non-fiction books, but the second editor disagreed and she changed my story from third person to first person and I am happy with the outcome of my first book. I want to clarify that I am not ashamed of who I am and where I have come from and that's why I am proud to share my story with others in the form of a book.

Beyond Calamity was initially published in December 2018 and my one hundred copies arrived at my home. As soon as I looked, touched and read the first page, I straight away realised that there was a big mistake with the book. I had to urgently send an email to stop the publisher from selling and printing the book until the mistake was fixed. The $1,000 I used to print the first hundred books went down the drain. I had to find more money to fix the mistake. After the mistake was fixed, my book was re-released in March 2019 and I couldn't be happier. The first editor had told me that my story was too big to fit in a novel so she asked me to divide the story into two, which I did, but when the book was first released it was so thin, seventy-eight pages only. I sent the other half of the story, which brought the book up to

152 pages. If I had given up, I would not have been able to write my second book.

People want to know how I did it and how long I had been writing before publishing my first book. Some people don't believe that *Beyond Calamity* is my first book. They think that this is probably my third book because of how well it is written. Did I join the book writing club and did I read the ten novels, as suggested? Absolutely not. In saying that, in July 2019, four months after *Beyond Calamity* was published, I joined the South Australian writers' club, not to learn how to write a book but to gain more knowledge of what services are available out there for South Australian writers and to also promote my book. Through Writers SA, I have been able to promote my book and sell a few copies. I have been able to register with Copyright Australia and I have also been able to link with Adelaide Festival for future Adelaide writers' events and see how I might be involved with those events in the future.

A big thank you to Fontaine Publishing Group, my second editor in particular, for editing my first book and for getting it out into the hands of my readers. My advice to anyone out there reading this book is that, if you have a talent, use it and never give up. If you want to publish that book you have been putting off, now is the time for you to do so, please go for it. If there seems to be no way of getting through it and you feel that you are about to give up, tell yourself that one more day, one more week, one more month, one more year and you will get there. You just need a little bit of patience, perseverance and lots of prayers along the way if you are a Christian and you will get there. Always remember that nothing good in life comes easy.

Esther's children, Destiny and Dorcas, laying down
on the floor on their tummies

Esther at a photo shoot in 2011

Destiny sitting in the backyard at home, enjoying beautiful
Adelaide weather in 2020

Dorcas at Godfreys' carpark in Adelaide

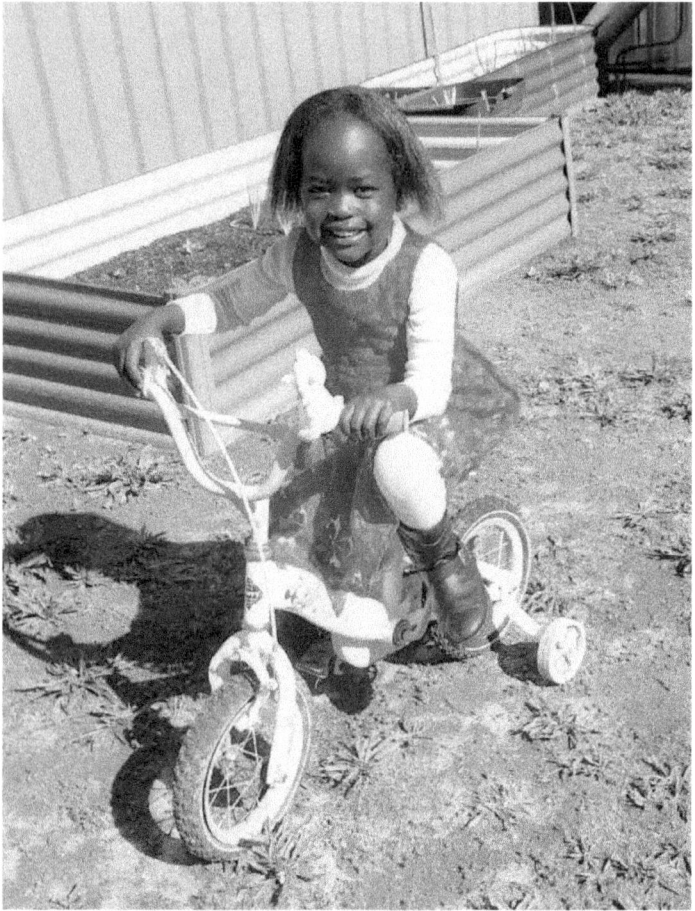
Dorcas riding her bike in the backyard at home

Esther and her daughters in their backyard at home in 2020

Esther at a professional photo shoot in 2011

www.ingramcontent.com/pod-product-compliance
Lightning Source LLC
Chambersburg PA
CBHW031949080426
42735CB00007B/318